Dancer

Dancer

Valerie Carpenter & Mark Osmun

CONTENTS

One	The Vision
Two	The Dancer
Three	Tombé a Terre
Four	Pollyanna
Five	Gravity
Six	The Ghost
Seven	First Movement
Eight	Second Movement
Nine	Solo
Ten	Cage Dancer
Eleven	Children of a Lesser God
Twelve	A Dancer's Gait
Thirteen	Downtime in the Rockies
Fourteen	Transition
Fifteen	Pause
Sixteen	Pas de Deux
Seventeen	Performance Enhancer
Eighteen	Dark Reprise
Nineteen	Dying Swan
Twenty	Crucible
Twenty-One	Limon
Twenty-Two	Freedom Dancing

Authors' Note

This book is based on the life of Valerie Glines Carpenter. It is a work of nonfiction, based on interviews, documents, photographs, resumes and depositions. Some literary license has been exercised. For example, because such a long timespan is covered, some events have been compressed or rendered out of sequence in the interest of story-flow. Also, since few, if any, conversations were ever recorded, the ones in this book are reconstructions based on participants' best recollections—always staying true to the spirit, message and tone of the dialogs—though, in many cases, not verbatim. Some persons' names have been omitted or altered for the sake of privacy and confidentiality.

One — The Vision

The strange trappings of an Intensive Care Unit surround the bed like a tangle of briars. All manner of medical apparatus loom over Valerie. She's gripped by a "halo" that looks like a medieval torture device with its pins screwed into her skull from a steel ring anchored to a plastic vest. A respirator with its mask and tubes that suggest some high-altitude test pilot, various IVs carrying drugs and saline, heart and oxygen monitors, articulated arms that lift a plethora of equipment over or away from the bed, denote the sudden paraphernalia of a spinal surgery patient.

But she doesn't see any of it. Rendered unconscious by pain, fatigue, trauma, shock, residual anesthesia, morphine and a varied cocktail of drugs flowing through her body, Valerie sees only the disconnected and wavering images of her opiated dreams.

Like figures in a mirage, people and settings shimmer and sway, glitter for a few seconds and then dissolve.

A cluster of students hunches in the corner of a gymnasium at Gallaudet College for the Deaf. The kids keep their eyes turned inward toward their own circle, their eyes following the fluid movements of each others' hands as they make private comments about the new student teacher who stands in the middle of the floor beckoning. One, then another looks up furtively in the teacher's direction, sees her wide smile, then retreats back into the group's private circle of vision. One of them, a young man in a shag-do and beginnings of a mustache, signs, "She had to spell out 'choreography.'" Some giggle awkwardly at that.

Actually, the woman's fluency with American Sign Language is not so bad; that's not the real issue. It's what she says. She invites these students to come to the center of the gym where she promises to instruct them in Modern Dance.

The students—even though all members of the college's Dance Club—know nothing about real dancing. Not a lesson between them. Until now, they've just turned up the music, felt the pulsing beat via the speakers, or coursing upward from the wooden floor right through their feet, and just flailed around as the spirit moved them. Now something different presents itself and they shift around uneasily, heads hunched, eyes toward the floor when they're not watching their own conversations.

The teacher, Valerie Glines, 24, a lithe figure in black tights, hair long and brown, moves to the stereo system—a huge arrangement of amps and speakers—and puts in an eight-track tape of Vicki Sue Robinson's Turn the Beat Around, *cranks the volume and bass up to the max, then glides, hops, bounces over to the knot of students.*

"Feel that?" she asks in sign, all the while bouncing up and down like a kid chomping at the bit to burst out the back door to go play. The students can't help but get caught in the slipstream of her roiling enthusiasm. One, then the other start to bob.

Except for one—the shag-haircut-and-lip-shadow student. The lone holdout looks at the floor. Valerie moves over to him, takes his hand. He looks up and she slowly signs: "I've been shy. It kept me from having fun. Then I realized: no one cares how I do*—they only care about how* they *do…No one's watching you. If you dance like no one's watching, you'll have nothing but fun."*

She smiles her ear-to-ear expression of joy, then turns to the group. "I'm Valerie. We're going to have fun."

With that she draws them toward the center of the floor —a Pied Piper procession, a few kids still hesitant, but shuffling along nonetheless.

The kids cluster around her at the center of the gym. She says, "Feel the beat? Okay? Now here's something weird I want you to try—using your body, in time to the beat, make the shape of a...horse."

Huh?

"Like this."

Valerie, a light, supple young woman who seemingly can bend in any direction, rolls her hands and arms in a hula-like motion, then her body follows, her head dipping and lunging forward in a regular loping rhythm.

The kids stare. Then they see the horse and are amazed that it actually looks...cool.

"Try it," Valerie beams that wide, perfect-toothed smile (never getting off the horse). "Just try. Try. Try. Try...There. That's it." She giggles.

The kids move, slowly at first—but that Valerie is so darn positive, so...upbeat—that their shoulders loosen, their heads swivel, their hips sway, their feet stamp, until they become something that resembles a timed stampede.

The kid in the shag and nascent milkshake-mustache canters up to Valerie. Still in dance mode, he hand-spells "choreography" then says, "Here's the sign," then holds his left hand open, palm up, forms a "C" with his right hand and wriggles it along the left hand's palm.

"And here's what your name looks like from now on," he declares and combines the sign for 'dance' with the letter "V".

The dancers fade away and for an indefinite time nothing exists until other random memories punctuate the darkness. In one stretch she tap-dances for her classmates at Churchill Road Elementary School in Virginia. In another, she sits in a room where her various diplomas hang—the Bachelors and Masters in dance, and the Masters in counseling. A deaf woman sits opposite her, recounting her troubles. Val listens intently. They hug. They disappear.

Next she sees her own older sister, Karen.

Summertime in Virginia where mown grass heavily scents the humid air. The swish of their swings keeps them cool, their bare feet pointing, with each arc, toward the sky. Karen points at Valerie's foot, toward an incredibly small freckle. "That's so ugly," she says. "No boy will ever love you with that." Val nearly falls off the swing. The action pulls her head backward so that it faces the sky. And now, she cranes her head upward to see.... the cliff dwellings at Montezuma Castle in Arizona.

How did the Indians get up there? What if they fell? she wonders. She magically ascends the cliffs and now crouches in a dry, tan cave, its ceiling charred black from ancient cook fires. A scorpion dashes across the floor. Valerie takes a step backward from it. She missteps. Her balance point shifts toward the edge. The canyon floor yawns hundreds of feet below. She falls. "It's over," she says. "No one will ever love me."

As she falls she sees a woman on the cliff above. The old woman, with fading reddish hair wrapped in a bun, wears the modest, puffed-sleeve, calico dress of an Oklahoma homesteader. Though hundreds of feet away and falling ever farther, Valerie clearly hears the woman say, "It's never over, Vaddie. Don't you ever quit...Love will find you."

Two — The Dancer

Mornings in the 1960s in the suburban home of Colonel Carroll V. Glines start promptly at 0600. The household rises and each individual attends to his or her specific duties. Valerie, the youngest, still in her robe, sets the breakfast table before returning to her quarters to dress. David, the middle child, collects the morning's *Washington Post* and sets it next to the Colonel's place. Karen, eight years older than Valerie, heats the kettle, then immediately claims her birthright primacy to the bathroom. Mrs. Glines, looking as fresh as the morning, appears in the kitchen and sets the three-ring circus of meals in motion—soft-boiled egg, coffee and toast for the Colonel, Cherrios cereal for David and Valerie, only toast for the figure-conscious Karen.

This being Saturday morning, the Colonel enjoys a leisurely breakfast, untroubled by his usual rush to his Pentagon post. When the full company assembles, all sit down together and only then dig in.

This morning, one of those glorious northern Virginia moments at the cusp between spring and summer, begs for fun. At this point, the area still rolls with farmlands dating back to Colonial times, and bathes in fragrances— honeysuckle, gardenias, magnolias—not to mention the newly-cut grass of the tract homes just beginning to dot the region. Maples, hardwoods, crab apples, pines, poplar, sassafras, dogwoods and redbuds turn the area into an expensive bouquet. Even the dirt smells rich.

After a night with the windows open—but not the screens—and Valerie's head still full of the sounds of crickets and owls, plus the hypnotic blinking of lightning bugs, she wakes to the crisp smell of dew on the grass and a concerto from cardinals and finches. She cannot wait to burst out the door and play.

But she will wait; no surprise there.

The troops have chores to do before being granted leave. David will take out the trash, then wash the cars, then mow the lawn. Karen will dust and vacuum before she goes anywhere. Valerie will clean the bathrooms.

Normally, the kids don't have a lot of interaction with their father. During the week he works, comes home, there's the dinner drill, then he writes.

Col. Carroll V. Glines, a prodigious writer, author of dozens of books on military history, all put out by major publishers, works incessantly. His most famous work is probably *Doolittle's Tokyo Raiders*, about the daring attack on Japan's capital just after Pearl Harbor.

So after dinner and on weekends Col. Glines settles in behind his Royal typewriter at a table strewn with notes—in the T.V. room—and writes. The kids don't mind so much that he doesn't play with them; they wouldn't know what that looked like. But the *T.V. room*... They can't watch tv or listen to records; they... must... be... quiet. Dad...is... writing.

But on weekends like this, with a little time to spare in the morning, the Colonel has time for them. Inspection.

The kids don't just have to complete their tasks before going out to play; their work must pass muster. Sometimes a visual inspection suffices. But for some tasks—dusting for instance—the Colonel runs a white handkerchief over a random flat piece of terrain to determine the thoroughness of Karen's work. He might use a toothpick to check for dirt remaining on the baseboards, or run an old toothbrush under the lip of the toilet bowl. When inspection concludes and all appears to be in order, the kids rejoice at the words, "Dismissed... I mean go play."

This is not to say that the Colonel is a martinet. By no means. He possesses only so much time and he understands, first-hand, the long-range benefits of discipline. Still, he finds time for the important things. He sits with Valerie at her homework table, explaining—to no avail—a trivial math problem about a train traveling at a certain rate of speed. He even sets up a salt-shaker to represent the train and napkin rings to represent the stations on the route, but Valerie looks at him blankly. He might as well try to explain the physics behind an Atlas rocket.

Less frustrating—but no less difficult—he asks Valerie, about to turn 10, what she wants for her August birthday and she—strangely—says she wants to walk up the Washington Monument, which you could do in those days, walk up all 897 steps of it. The summer temperature hits 90 degrees and 90 percent humidity, but they do it.

Still, for good or ill, family life at the Glines encampment runs more on regimented schedules and tasks, than on intimacy or fun.

Being military, the Glines family uproots itself at short intervals. Oklahoma. Alabama. Ohio. Virginia. Alaska. Back to Virginia.

Making friends presents a challenge for the kids. Just about the time you forge friendships, an unwelcome governmental hand yanks you somewhere else. You lose your entire friend-network. You start all over—which is never easy, right? Kids, being kids, often turn a cold shoulder to newcomers. And in the back of your mind, something says why bother? You're going to all this effort and for what? Leave the new friends behind in another couple of years? Go through it over and over?

Valerie's mother knows all about this. She knows that the best way for her kids to make friends, to shorten the transitional lonely period to a bare minimum, is sign them up for activities.

Dance lessons (and piano lessons—her mother having been a concert-quality pianist) begin for Valerie in second grade.

At first, the dance lessons take place in the cafeteria of Churchill Road Elementary. A teacher from the James School of the Dance Arts, visits after school one day a week. The kids push the lunch tables back, giving them a temporary 30 x 50-foot square of linoleum as their first dance floor.

Looking back, Valerie says, "I loved it right away. Dancing was freedom. Freedom from school, from homework, freedom from…my home. I was free to move in ways that weren't normal; to do what I wanted… It's simple: I'm free to be me," she says. "Free to interpret the music any way I want. Free to move through space. Let loose……free from inhibitions. Turns out, I was good at it. There was actually something I was good at—and people said so. It became my thing, then my life."

So after dance class, after chores, before homework, and before Dad comes home and dinner arrives, Valerie dances around the house, practicing. She sometimes pauses and tunes in *The Mickey Mouse Club* show—5 p.m. WRC-TV — where the Mouseketeers sing and dance periodically throughout the production. Soon after, she writes—in careful, hand-printed pencil characters, (she hasn't learned cursive yet) —to Jimmie Dodd, the adult ringleader of the group:

Dear Mr. Dodd,

My name is Valerie Glines. I live in Virginia. I am eight years old. I love to dance. I would like to be a Mouseketeer on your show. May I come to Los Angeles and audition?

Sincerely,

Valerie Glines

He actually writes back. The copies are long gone now, but nothing comes of it anyway and the girl says to herself, in a Pollyanna sort of way, that Mr. Dodd must be a very busy man and the delay will just give her time to become an even better dancer.

Otherwise she watches Shirley Temple and Fred Astaire/Ginger Rodgers movies. She sneaks out to see the dancing in the movie *Viva Las Vegas*; sneaks out because Mom views Elvis and Ann Margaret as almost pornographic.

"Dance was my happiness," Valerie recalls. "Dance always presented a challenge to get better... to be able to do more turns at a time, a deeper plié, lift my legs higher, jump higher, push my limits."

By the end of the school year, Valerie's parents view her love of dance as genuine: no passing fancy. They sign her up for the actual James School of the Dance—located one floor above a Baskins Robbins, just around the corner from Giant Grocery. The school offers more variety of classes than the Churchill Elementary cafeteria version and Valerie takes them all: ballet, jazz, tap.

Fast forward, past classes with the Washington (D.C.) Ballet, the school recitals, the move to Alaska, the Anchorage Civic Ballet, the high school productions of *Oklahoma* and *Annie Get Your Gun*, college at Arizona State where she learns the techniques of Martha Graham... fast forward to the Boston Conservatory, where Valerie transfers in 1972 because of its similarity to Juilliard and its total focus on molding future entertainers in singing, dance, acting, musicianship. Total immersion. Dancers there learn all the arts—dance, music, singing, acting. You audition to get in.

The school is not some pastoral green campus with a frisbee-crossed quad and students leisurely strolling through their illusory Utopia. Valerie faces an urban school, about 600 yards as the crow flies from home plate at Fenway Park and about 190 yards from the middle of the Massachusetts Turnpike. Founded in 1867, it's the oldest performing arts school in America. Its primary building sits on a short, one-way side street. Not a particularly welcoming structure—a stern, layered, granite face at street-level with narrow, vertical rectangles for windows; a second floor of brick with six wide, arched windows; a squatty top level of brick with four rectangular window ports capped with false-front triangles that face you like raised eyebrows. The Boston Conservatory: hard-nosed, old, Big Time, hard core—and that's the way she wants it. At the same time, the school sits within the city's "artistic" district—fortune tellers, street musicians, cafes, long-hairs in Renaissance-style rigs (authentic except for the tie-dyed colors). Boston's version of Haight-Ashbury, very hip.

But the area's hipster affectations hold little attraction for Valerie. She dances most of the day; rehearses late into the night; patches her blisters, rubs Ben-Gay on her sore muscles and goes to bed smiling.

In late-January 1972, slush sullies Boston's streets and frost outlines every window of the dance studio, framing the alley below and giving it an usually charming look. Within, Valerie's choreographer instructor presents the students with the semester's assignment: create a dance, based on a poem or written piece of music, at least six minutes in length—otherwise, no constraints—it must be composed, rehearsed, performed and judged 28 days hence. Go.

Hours later, Valerie stares out her dorm room window, across the turnpike to the Conservatory. The Conservatory, lacking enough dorm space of its own, contracts with Grahm Junior College across the Turnpike to house some of its students in a barely resurrected former hotel. From her room, Valerie sees both the Conservatory and Fenway Park which at that time of year sit under a layer of snow.

No creative answers present themselves on the bleak winterscape. She turns away and flops on the bed, staring at the ceiling. Forget poetry… So it'll be music. But what? A bad choice now and everything else in the assignment goes down the tubes, which could mean that everything else in life —a future as a dancer, or a choreographer, Broadway, Hollywood—might go down with it.

She closes her eyes and breathes deeply—exhausted, not only by the normal routine of dance, but by the stress of the new creative demand.

In her dream she wanders into a dimly lighted auditorium. A banner hangs on one of the walls: "GO SAXONS." Someone plays a piano. Off to one side of the otherwise empty stage she sees the instrument and at its keyboard a young man—a teenager in thick, black-framed glasses, dark wavy hair and sideburns going long below his ears. The music sounds much older than the boy. Its upwellings and fall-offs speak of some angst that perhaps high schoolers shouldn't know. Then it dances up lightly, a bright surge of joy that brings thoughts of flight and freedom to her ears. Then it becomes seductive, sexy. Then violent. Then returns to the beginning.

She recognizes him: her short-term boyfriend at Langley High School. He's playing the same piece as when they met. In fact, it's the same scene as when they met.

She glides over to the piano.

"No, don't stop," she says when he sees her and pauses.

But he stops anyway and looks down. His face reddens.

"I'm just… it's not like I'm supposed to be here…This is just a really good piano…I can come back later."

"No. No, stay. I'm not exactly supposed to be here either. Just thought I'd practice my dance thing. I'm in the musical… Shoot, I can dance and you can just go on playing. You sound great."

He blushes again. "I'm John."

"I'm Valerie."

He looks at her and says, "I know."

The dream wakes her up. All of that happened two years ago—ages in youthful time. She had dated John Carpenter for only a couple of months when a misunderstanding ruined everything. It started off great. Then there was a make-out session—nothing heavy, just kissing really. Elated and naive, John told a friend about it later, but did not understand the terminology and confused "making out" with "making love." Word got back to Valerie and, being a good girl who placed a very high value on reputation, that was that.

John withdrew into his music. Losing young love hurts anyone, but losing it on a misunderstanding, and being a sensitive, artistic type, made this an especially searing time for him. He wrote a song about it, a beautiful, plaintive melody with lyrics that, many years later, will seem prescient. The song later reaches #3 on sales charts in Michigan:

Princess of a Fool

There she is.
She's the princess of a fool.
She may know what she's looking for,
But somehow this won't do.

So there she is
With my whole world at her feet
She can have anything she wants
But her needs I can't meet.

(Chorus)
So what can I do to please her?
What can I do to ease her?
And how can I say without shame,

That my life, 'cause of her, was rearranged?

She tried not to think about him ever since; tried not to entertain the notion that she'd made a hasty and harsh judgment and maybe missed out on something special.

She wonders if the dream came to her because of the pressure of the choreography assignment, or if she should merely add it to a long line of John-dreams that plague her periodically.

"It's the music," she says aloud. "Definitely."

She stands up, walks over to the phone, calls Virginia Information and asks for John Carpenter's number—or more precisely, his parents' number. She writes it down but then doesn't call it.

She imagines how the conversation might go.

Hi John. It's Valerie…Click. No it wouldn't go like that.

Hi John. It's Valerie. How are you?…Good. Me too… In Boston. I'm at the Conservatory, studying dance. You?… Actually, that's what I'm calling about. I need some music and I love yours so much…

She takes a breath, hits the keys on the phone, listens to it ring, then hangs up.

Right. I haven't seen or heard from him in two years and now I want a favor… but it would be good to talk to him anyway. Right? Music or not… Right? Okay.

She hits the keys again and this time waits. On the fourth ring, someone picks up.

"Hello?"

"Oh, ah. Hi, John. It's Valerie."

* * *

At four years old, John Carpenter doodles with crayons as his two sisters bang their way through piano lessons in the Carpenter living room.

The girls have been taking lessons for some time, but do not seem to be into it—and Mrs. Holloway, their teacher, mentions this to their mother.

"I know. I know," Mrs. Carpenter sighs. "I can't get them to practice."

"That's enough, girls," the patient Mrs. Holloway says, signaling an end to the torment.

The girls shrug and immediately head for the door, pausing only to dart into the kitchen for cookies.

"Perhaps, some time off would do them good," Mrs. Holloway offers.

"Perhaps."

Mrs. Carpenter sighs and pulls out a checkbook for this week's lessons, then stops as the room suddenly fills with the powerful chords and melody of the *Doxology*.

The women turn to see the boy, legs dangling off the edge of the piano bench, hands barely wide enough to hit a full chord, running through the hymn without so much as one error.

Mrs. Holloway turns toward Mrs. Carpenter, mouth agape.

Mrs. Carpenter shrugs and smiles in an embarrassed rather than boastful way.

"He plays all the time… We get home from church, he sits down and plays all the songs we sang that day."

"No lessons?"

"Not yet."

There's a long pause. Mrs. Holloway takes a deep breath as if stockpiling fuel for a big speech.

"Mrs. Carpenter, please don't take offense, but I must say you're wasting your money on the girls' lessons. Let me teach your son instead."

John starts lessons with Mrs. Holloway the next week. The lessons only last a month. At that point Mrs. Holloway calls to tell Mrs. Carpenter that John, at four years old, is too far advanced for her tutelage to do much good. She refers the Carpenters to a Mrs. Trebert at The Eastman School of Music, part of the University of Rochester.

Mrs. Carpenter calls Mrs. Trebert and mentions the referral.

"I don't work with children," Mrs. Trebert explains, "Especially a child who is only four years old. I work at the college or with older students privately at my home."

But Mrs. Carpenter begs for an audition at least and finally Mrs. Trebert grudgingly agrees to a short listen on the following Tuesday.

At the appointed time, John crawls up on the piano bench and plays a Bach *Two-Part Invention*.

When the final note fades, Mrs. Trebert says, "We shall start next Wednesday at 3:30 and we will have regular weekly lessons."

After several weeks of instruction, Mrs. Trebert sits the boy down for a talk.

"John, there's a new song I'd like you to try."

"Okay," he grins. "Um…. could you play it for me first so I can hear how it is supposed to sound?"

Mrs. Trebert plays Chopin's *Grande Valse Brilliante*. John listens carefully.

When she finishes, Mrs. Trebert spreads the sheet music on the stand in front of her pupil and taps on the pages. "Now you."

The boy grins, gives a cursory look at the music, then plays the piece perfectly.

To the boy's amazement, the teacher doesn't smile or praise him; instead, she squints, like someone concerned or perplexed.

She says, "You don't read music do you?"

He looks down at the floor.

"Didn't I play it right?..I can try it again."

"You played beautifully. It was perfect," she says. Then she taps the sheet music, "Except that this music in front of you is a completely different piece… You're just playing by ear and memory, aren't you?"

He nods, still looking down. "I don't understand the notes. They don't make sense to me."

Over a decade later, a physician diagnoses his dyslexia.

* * *

By sheer coincidence, John and his Langley High School friend and rock bandmate, Jon Chase, are planning a scouting trip to Boston from Virginia at the time Valerie calls. Jon Chase, the drummer in their high school band, *The Incredible Fog*, has been accepted to the Berklee School of Music, located virtually next to the Conservatory. Both of them plan to move to Boston that fall. Neither have any idea, until Valerie's phone call, that their classmate and John's one and only crush now lives there.

The two arrive at Valerie's dilapidated dorm a week later. Jon Chase offers to wait in the lobby—just in case something develops between Valerie and John. John goes upstairs and follows directions to Valerie's door where he waits for a while and assesses the dingy surroundings. It's as if the building says, "You want to be an artist? Then get used to this." John hears tinny music and garbled conversation going on inside; he can't make it out partly because everyone talks at once, and partly because an ear infection from a couple of years ago rendered him deaf in one ear.

He already knows that this reunion will not be a huggy one, not on his part anyway. Sure, he told Valerie he'd be happy to provide music for her; his personal code demands that much. But he has his pride and the breakup stings even now. Still, the fact remains that he's reworked one of his earlier compositions—*The Serpent*—wrote a new prelude and new ending for it, trimmed it to match the six-minute length Valerie requires, and recorded it in a studio for her.

He knocks on the door with one hand and holds the five-inch reel-to-reel tape in the other. The door opens slowly and not completely. Valerie peers out. She smiles faintly, awkwardly—the weirdness of being young, the hangover of high school still lingering between them. Behind her, five students prattle about some teacher they have in common.

"Hi," she says.

"Hi."

"I'd invite you in but…" She waves a hand toward the group.

"No problem. Here's your tape. Hope you like it."

"Um, yes. I'm sure I will. Thank you, John."

He hands her the tape. The door closes. That's it.

John can't believe she's snubbed him after all he's done. It's just so… cold.

He tries to reconcile his image of the perfect girl with this icy treatment. She's better than that, he thinks. What he can't suspect—given his idealized image of Valerie—is that his perfect lady has flaws. In fact, she shares with him the same afflictions: extreme social awkwardness and shyness rooted in low self-esteem. She turned him away simply because she lacks the social skills needed to make a meeting like this one smooth.

Because Valerie will leave the Conservatory at the end of the semester and John won't move to Boston until a few months after that, it will be almost 20 years before they see each other again.

***

The Serpent, John's composition for Valerie's dance, reveals itself as a masterful, rich and complex piano piece. Some will say, while admitting that words fall short, that the piece starts out slowly, its notes dropping like small beads of water onto steel plates, or perhaps evoking images of a light snowfall. Then a deeper counterpoint arrives, adding a sense of concern. The rhythm changes. The chords become heroic, suggesting a struggle, a quest of some sort. Then it brightens and bounces: perhaps a merry chase through a countryside, until it finally slows again and returns to its contemplative, peaceful beginning.

To Valerie the music suggests a narrative of a love triangle whose theme will have to do with the choice between "Advance and Retreat."

There will be three dancers: two women and a man—that much Valerie knows. But what they will do, how they will move, what plot line will be shown, all those things float in the air above her bed at night and change with every minute. She finds that once you start making choices, the fewer options remain, and the possibilities narrow from there. One wrong choice and you travel down a dead end. So she hesitates making any choices at all. She stops thinking and lets the music move through her.

John Carpenter's music—since that first day in the Langley auditorium—feels to her like an innate part of her anatomy; or like some important memory she'd forgotten and then miraculously remembers. No other music has ever been like that for her. She lets the sounds inform her decisions.

She chooses a young student named Heather to play the lead. Heather looks like an angel: a perfectly oval face framed by thick, dark hair, a dancer's body of course, and a broad sweet smile. Naturally, she will represent Good.

Valerie will play against type. She will be the evil temptress—a challenge for her. Her character will use her wiles attempting to seduce Heather's true love.

Ten days pass. Just over two weeks remain before the performance. The three dancers rehearse every day and often late into the night. Mistakes dot every rehearsal. The clock on the wall now does more than tell time; it subtracts time. Every minute, every passing second brings them closer to the Day of Judgment. But Valerie tells herself that mistakes are good. *Better to have mistakes now than later. Mistakes show them what needs to be fixed. Yes, mistakes are good; everything is good. Keep telling yourself that or you'll lose it.*

Judgment Day, otherwise known as the Performance, arrives during a rare break in the weather—a rogue spring-like afternoon in early March. The first dances begin at nine a.m. They've scheduled Valerie's performance for four in the afternoon.

Rather than go now and watch the other dances, Valerie sits in her room and chews at her nails. She gets up, goes to the window, finds nothing to distract her, paces the room, goes to the bed and lies on it, looking straight up. For the thousandth time she sees the performance in her head, imagines what the audience will see. She considers throwing up—but no, that would be a concession to nervousness, to a lack of confidence. Instead, she sits up abruptly, puts on a big smile.

"This is going to be the best day of your life," she declares to the empty room. "Yes, it is… You can't wait. It's going to be great. Let's go."

She gets up, assembles her gear and heads for the auditorium four hours early.

Off stage, peering out at the audience, Valerie hears her piece being introduced. Her damp hands clench and unclench. She swallows, or at least tries to—her throat doesn't seem to be working right. But then John's music begins and right away it's like having a friend beside her, a friend so confident in you that you feel it too. She feels the muscles in her neck relax. She shakes the tension from her hands. The music becomes the moment. A student stagehand pauses near her and she gives him—unlike her in real life—a sly, sexy grin.

The male character enters from stage left. He moves with hesitation, each foot placed carefully in front of the other. He moves his head from side to side, for a time not finding what he seeks. Then his angel arrives.

Light, bright, full of welcoming love and joy, the angel embraces him. They move as one. He lifts her high. She soars without effort. Their bodies entwine—not so much with lust as with union.

A rhythmic shift in the music arrives: Valerie's cue. Without even thinking about it, she appears onstage, dancing toward the pair. She circles them, hardly seeming to touch the ground. She inserts herself between the two lovers. She pulls him away from his true love. He resists. His angel comes to his side. The evil one slides between them and snakes her way up his torso. The angel pulls her away. She sweeps in again from the other side. At one point the three squirm like entangled snakes, difficult to say where one begins and another stops. The three take a wild ride on the music, each advancing and retreating.

At one point, he lifts Valerie high above the stage and seems to throw her into space. An illusion manifests itself: Valerie's demon falls hard to the ground before getting up again, only to be thrown high once more. Airborne, Valerie, the dancer, tastes freedom. She hears sighs from her audience, but staying in character, suppresses a smile.

Finally, the angel, heartbroken, retreats from the scene. Having won, the evil temptress abandons her prize, who now broods alone about everything he has lost and where it all went wrong.

The lights dim as the music fades.

When the lights come on again, the audience applauds, hoots, whistles its approval. The three performers prance back to center stage. Valerie's smile stretches out so big she feels it might break her face. A small tear of relief trickles from the corner of her eye. She's given them a flawlessly-performed, perfect marriage of sight and sound.

She knows she's created the best thing she's ever done.

Three — Tombé a Terre

Valerie Daniell (her last name now leftover from a divorce) sits behind the wheel of her white 1998 Subaru Outback, two peoples' gear stowed beneath the hatchback, rolling across Highway 10 in southern Arizona, heading west toward Tucson. It's open country here. Substantial mountains —nothing compared to the ones she left behind yesterday in Colorado, but burly nonetheless—flank her route, lying a good ten miles to her right, to the north. Otherwise, it's undulating, open Sonoran desert: few towns, few cars, just a massive blue sky and a landscape of saguaros, the yellow-blossoms of palo verde trees and the occasional sculpture-like piles of tanned and massive boulders for visual relief. In places, the highway straightens out toward a distant horizon that suggests the endless possibilities of life and of her life in particular. March 2000: the temperatures are cool, the air fragrant with...*what is that? Creosote bush maybe? Not the same thing as creosote, the tar. No, this has a sweet perfume to it... Did I wear perfume at that presentation? Can't remember. No, I didn't. That would have been a bad idea. Unprofessional.*

The Presentation and the wide open spaces are apt companions today. They both represent an unlimited future —where the possibilities, the potential of everywhere she's been and everything she's done so far, are coming together like the lines of perspective drawn down this long highway.

Since college, now so long ago, she'd accumulated skills—at first glance disparate and unrelated skills, but now part of a single package about to bud into something outstanding. The resume shows fluency in American Sign

Language, work as an interpreter, a Masters degree in dance, directing a dance company for the deaf called "Deafinite Motion", a Masters degree in counseling, a license in psychotherapy, running a K-12 Counseling Program in Denver, counseling at the Colorado School for the Deaf and Blind, running a private practice counseling individuals, families, children and couples; consulting to University of Colorado Hospital's Department of Audiology, and presenting on "The Psychological Aspects of Deafness and Cochlear Implants on Children" to the staff at the Mayo Clinic in Scottsdale, Arizona.

Right after that presentation, Valerie and the group of ten doctors, audiologists and staff from the presentation, left the conference room, moved past the grand piano in the Clinic's lobby, to the cafeteria for lunch. On the way, the head of Audiology shook Valerie's hand and said, "So nice to meet you…When can you start?"

Huh?

"We want to start up a counseling program for our patients—and a program to counsel parents and children to see if they are good candidates for the implants. I think you fit the bill—you could run it."

Over lunch Valerie heard a sales pitch for the many benefits of working at the Mayo Clinic (*Right. You had me at "When can you start?"*)—the low cost of living in Arizona, the nine months of perfect weather, the employee benefits, the prestige, and a raft of other items which passed Valerie's semi-dazed brain unnoticed. She had simply expected to deliver a talk. No one told her anything about a job being offered. She left lunch flattered and excited, but would like to think about it. They agreed to keep in touch in the coming weeks.

Valerie flew back to Denver the same day and told her boyfriend about the possible job.

"You'd be moving to Arizona?" he asked.

"Well, yes—if I got the job and took it."

A long pause, then, "Whatever."

In the weeks that followed, Valerie exchanged emails with the department head regarding salary, starting dates, the usual stuff. She arranged to visit Scottsdale that March to scout out the housing market.

So now she's on her way. She thinks, "It's all coming together."

Valerie leans her head out the window and breathes the air of coming opportunities.

"Could you roll that up?" Her boyfriend jerks his thumb toward the window. "It's getting chilly."

She complies immediately. They drive in silence—just as they have for the last two hours—then Valerie brightens and says, "How about some Eagles? They kind of fit here, don't you think?"

She's suggesting the music of the The Eagles, not so much because they fit the landscape (although they do), but because she knows *he* loves The Eagles and maybe their music would improve the vibe a little. In fact, the offering of Eagles might be seen as symbolic of this whole trip.

In Santa Fe, they had hit the southwestern artisan shops, the Palace of the Governors, and the pueblo of Cafe Pasqual's—named for the folk saint of Mexican and New Mexican kitchens.

Even before tasting the food, Pascual's entertains with its murals by Leovigildo Martinez and with its hand-painted Mexican tiles. *The food, now that should do it. He'll love the fresh baked bread, the home-made chile sauces, the hash.* Pasqual's will get the trip off to the right start, and that's important because the whole plan of the trip itself—the New Mexico detour, the extra days checking out Tucson, then going even further off-course to hike within the Organ Pipe Cactus National Park in southwestern Arizona (he loves hiking) where they will see people with backpacks and children entering the country, the ride north again to Phoenix and Scottsdale to drive around, look at neighborhoods (but not with a realtor as that might bring things into too sharp a focus), then up to picturesque Sedona for hiking among the famed Red Rocks (he loves hiking, you know)—the whole plan of this entire odyssey has been simply to make the idea of her taking the Mayo job more palatable to him. Maybe he'll think about joining her.

But if Valerie takes the job at Mayo, that's it. He can't move, even if he wants to. He has kids and a job in Denver. Theoretically he could get another job, but commuting to Denver—two days by car, or too many dollars by plane—to see his kids, well that's a deal-breaker. So, while Valerie sees the trip as a way to perhaps warm him to the idea, he's likely seeing it as the Farewell Tour.

"No. Let's just enjoy the quiet," he says, leaving the cassette on the console between them. The Eagles do not get to sing *Already Gone*.

They scout Scottsdale quickly. It looks nice. The serrated ridge of Thompson Peak, crowned by huge antennae, overlooks the northern neighborhoods near the Clinic, not too far from Frank Lloyd Wright's architectural cult at Taliesin West, not too far from the equestrian mecca at WestWorld. Clean. Affluent. A little Utopia. But Valerie keeps these assessments to herself for now.

"Are we done?" he asks as they drive past the Clinic.

"Sure," Valerie forces a smile. "On to Sedona."

Heading north on Highway 17, they climb 2,000 feet in just a few minutes. The road lifts and winds, leaving the developed Phoenix area so quickly as to suggest the city never existed. Instead, deep canyons, sprawling cattle ranches, and the Mogollon (pronounced Mug-E-On) Rim—a 200-mile wide escarpment that forms the southern edge of the Colorado Plateau—materialize in its place. The road not only twists, it climbs and drops. They're up past 5,000 feet, then down to 3,000, then up to 4,000. The saguaros and the

Sonoran desert stop as they climb the Rim. From one crest they can look down a seven-mile long, six percent grade opening onto the green, expansive valley of Camp Verde. She keeps her eyes on the road, but for him a breathtaking vista unfolds. They come into the valley and take a short side trip before going on to Sedona.

Not far from Camp Verde, just up Beaver Creek, the ruins of the misnamed "Montezuma Castle" perch within its desert cliffs. The Sinagua people first inhabited the place 900 years earlier. The visitors park at the trailhead and walk the short, one-third mile, paved trail to just below the ancient five-story, stacked pueblo structures which blend into massive cavities 100 feet above.

"Awesome," Valerie says. "Imagine climbing up and down that every day."

"Helluva commute... We should go. Check in at the motel, see what's what in Sedona."

They leave and soon are on the awesome approach to Sedona. Each curve unveils a new geological wonder—the Red Rock cliffs, the "Bell," a pyramid-shaped formation found in every tourist's album, "Snoopy," a ridge formation that resembles Charlie Brown's dog lying on the roof of its doghouse. At every bend, signs point out the obvious: "Scenic View Point." Numerous pullouts dot the road, each offering trailheads and hiking. He loves hiking.

"This should be good," he says. "Awesome country." At last. Now a little hope for some real enjoyment peeks out. Maybe things will change.

They check into a Days Inn, then spend the remainder of the day walking around the tourist part of town —shops, galleries, t-shirts, bars, restaurants. She buys a turquoise necklace. They go to a fine restaurant for dinner which, oddly enough, has Trivial Pursuit cards in cups on the table. They play the game as they wait for their meals. They laugh.

This thing could turn around. Tomorrow will be great. Get up early, see the famous sunrise over the Red Rocks, take a hike, maybe wade around Oak Creek. Can't wait.

Sometime before dawn, Valerie wakes in the pitch black—the hotel curtains doing their job, with perhaps the help of rain clouds that moved in just before they went to bed, making things even more dark than normal. She wonders about the time, but the room has no lighted clock. She'd been so excited by the prospects of the next day, that she'd forgotten to leave a light on in the bathroom as she usually does. But she feels hunger: a sign that sunrise lurks nearby and that they should rise too if they hope to see the first rays. Besides, the motel serves free coffee and donuts in the lobby, so there's that incentive to get up in the dark.

She sits up, both legs tucked under her. She pushes up with her left hand on the mattress, so as to free her legs and starts to turn. She reaches out with her right hand for support on that side as she twists up and around. But there's nothing there; her right hand finds only empty space. In the blackness she hasn't realized that she'd been at the bed's lower edge. The hand pushes down into nothing and her body, in mid-turn, feet still tangled, drops backward.

There's a moment when time slows down enough, or one's brain speeds up enough, that creates a suspended moment during a crisis. A rush of vertigo means a backward fall—not too different from some dance moves, but now no one controls this one. She'll hit the floor—she knows it. She knows it will probably hurt, but she'll roll somehow on a shoulder and, other than embarrassment, an explanation, and some bruises, the morning will move on.

Yet she doesn't roll on a shoulder; she lands head-first. She hears a high-calibre rifle's booming crack. Her neck.

A blinding pain ricochets through her head and spine. She goes to move, but cannot. She has no feeling nor even

34

awareness of her own arms or legs. She may as well try to move someone else's limbs. The word "paralyzed" creeps before her. She pushes it away.

She calls out to him. He's already up, flips on the lights.

"Help me. I can't move."

"My God," he says. He stares for a second before undoing his own paralysis. He grabs the room phone, dials 911. It doesn't work. He dials 9, then 911. That doesn't work. Then 0, 911. Nothing.

"Going to the lobby. Calling 911. Hang on," he blurts before bolting out the door.

Now she sees the calling card of Panic and starts to babble.

"Hurry. Please. I can't breathe. I'm going to die. Tell my family I love them... This can't be happening."

In what seems like seconds, he's back. He drops a blanket over her.

"Help is coming. Stay calm."

"I can't die. I am not ready yet. Oh my God—I can't breathe."

"Everything's fine," he says, even though he doubts it.

She blacks out and so, remembers little—just bits and pieces like a slideshow with long, darkened pauses between each image.

Paramedics hover around her. Then blackness. The boxy interior of an ambulance... Then blackness... Shivers. Then black... She asks for morphine. Black... Pain. Black... Terror... Black... Sound of a jackhammer near her ears... Black... In a casket, a loud casket... somewhere a construction crew drills near her grave.... Black.

Everything changes. Just that fast.

Four — Pollyanna

Days later, after surgery in Flagstaff, Arizona, a special transport team takes her to Dallas, Texas to the Baylor Medical Center. But she doesn't know it.

The whole process—the surgery, the transfer, the admission, everything—exists only in snippets of images and sounds; hard to pinpoint whether they're memories or dreams. As before, she lies in a bed: a hospital bed, that much she knows.

She thinks back. She remembers Sedona. The fall. The fear. She recalls being in *some* hospital room, but not this one. She remembers seeing someone she knew as a child. A nurse. Her name tag said "Mariel."

"I knew a girl named Mariel." Valerie said in a dreamy voice. "Where are you from?"

"Virginia."

It dawned on her. The sister of her childhood best friend, Lori, floated before her.

"Are you Mariel...Fuller?"

A shock of recognition from the nurse. "Yes. Oh my God. Valerie."

"Your sister and I used to babysit you..."

That's all she remembers of the encounter and cannot say if she merely dreamed it. Wait... something else... She recalls her boyfriend of the past four years being by the bed. He's telling her he's not staying. He's got to see his kids. He says she should "hang in there." Then he's gone.

"I'm confused," she mutters, then closes her eyes and drifts off again. When she wakes, there's a doctor standing next to the bed, holding a phone.

"Where am I?"

"The Baylor Medical Center in Dallas," he says.

Thinking it a coincidence, she mutters, "My parents live in Dallas."

"Here." The doctor puts the telephone receiver against her ear. "It's your father."

She hears the Colonel's voice; it sounds tender, unusually so. "Hi sweetie, this is Dad... I'm so—"

"What happened?"

"Be sure to do what the doctor says. Okay?"

In what seems ages later, she wakes again and notices that the window ledge to the right of her bed supports an array of flowers. Did someone die? Her sister Karen sits nearby. Karen's husband, Ken, pushes a plastic spoon, laden with ice chips toward Valerie's mouth. She opens. The chips go in, cold, wet, welcomed. She tries to say something but words don't come.

The next time she wakes, her family stands around the bed: both parents, sister Karen and her husband, their son and his wife, their daughter and her husband. Her nephew stands at the end of the bed. He rubs her feet. She can see him doing it, but she can't feel it. Yet even if she could easily speak, she wouldn't tell him that his efforts are wasted and thus hurt his feelings.

That slide vanishes, replaced by another. In this one, she sees Karen putting socks and shoes on her and can't imagine why she's being made to wear shoes in bed... but nothing has made sense for so long she just mentally shrugs off this latest Wonderland weirdness. Next, people are putting her on a hard table. The table tilts upward. Her head spins.

"I'm afraid," she says.

"It's okay," says Karen.

The morphine kicks in again.

In time, the opiates subside enough for her to wake with a relatively clear mind. Unfortunately the odds of that moment coinciding with seeing an entourage of loved ones are slim. She wakes up alone and shivers. Her bed angles upward. Her eyes travel down her body. She sees a long cast-like sheath encasing her from neck to waist. She sees her hand and tries to move her fingers. Nothing—like someone else's hands lie there. Same with the arms and legs. She wonders if the neck-to-waist restraint has something to do with it. If only.

The fact remains: she can't move. It must be the brace: like being caught in the windings of a mummy, or strapped into a straight-jacket. Her breaths come in quick, short gasps. Her heartbeat picks up. She can't struggle or flail against her trappings. She opens her mouth to scream when a nurse walks in.

"Hi. I'm Sue. I'm one of your nurses." Sue wears a cheery, welcoming smile as if there's nothing wrong and she's a flight attendant about to take drink orders.

Valerie smothers her panic and tries to grin back, but can't be sure of the result. "No one's told me what's happened."

"Oh. Well, let's see… You had an accident in Arizona. You fractured your neck. You had surgery there. Then you were transferred here for rehab."

Rehab. The word carries with it all the hope in the world. I've been injured. Okay. Now I'm going to be fixed.

"How long will it take?"

Sue takes too long to answer. When she does, she's lost the flight attendant cheerfulness. "That's hard to say. It varies with the individual… I can tell you most people stay here around three months."

"And then they're better?"

Another pause. "Better than when they arrived… Most of them. We'll be getting you into rehab very soon."

"I dreamed my family was here."

"No, not a dream. They were here—just not right now… Listen, I've got to go. Good to meet you. Your breakfast will be here in a few minutes."

Sue leaves and sure enough, within a few minutes, an orderly appears with a tray upon which sits an array of scrambled eggs, bacon, a honeydew melon and a banana. The orderly puts the tray on a roll-over platform, slides it in front of Valerie, smiles, says, "Have a nice day," then leaves.

Valerie stares at the tray. What are they thinking? I can't move a muscle. How am I supposed to eat this? She takes a deep breath… Don't get upset. Someone will come and help with this. They have it covered.

But they don't.

The eggs, bacon, melon and banana sit there, inches away—as nearby as her past and just as unreachable.

Hours go by and no one appears. Nothing to do but look at the food and marvel at the ridiculousness of the situation. Valerie laughs—a sort of bitter chuckle—but even that minor relief gets cut short by a pain that sears through her neck.

When she thinks about it, she almost laughs again: she, a psychotherapist, has to appreciate the irony—some negative Pavlovian conditioning at work here… Doc, it only hurts when I laugh. But this time she doesn't laugh; the conditioning having taken its effect. She turns her gaze away from the food (if only she could avert her sense of smell) and counts the holes in the acoustic tiles above.

Time drags on and now she feels the need to blow her nose. Of course. Now this. But this time Providence intervenes. Another nurse arrives, this one to take her vital signs. Hallelujah.

"Thank God," Valerie says. "I need to blow my nose, can you help me?"

The nurse wriggles her own nose in a scrunchy smile. "Oh, I'm not very good at that…There's another nurse who is though. I'll get her to come."

When the nurse leaves, Valerie starts to cry. This, of course, makes the runny nose situation all the worse. She tells herself to stop crying, but she can't.

The nose-blowing specialist never shows up.

After a few hours, Valerie, exhausted, falls asleep. When she again wakes, the food tray has disappeared and her nose seems dry.

The next day, a new nurse pops in and introduces herself. She helps with the nose and gives Valerie a hand with the food. They chit-chat about the weather.

Then she says, "My husband and I have talked about your situation."

How nice: she actually cares, takes the work home with her.

She goes on. "If either of us became paralyzed, we'd kill ourselves. No way we could live like this."

Valerie marvels, stunned and silent as she wonders if another morphine-induced dream has replaced reality. A nurse could not have said that.

She has no reply for several moments, but then manages, "Thank you for blowing my nose." A few more seconds go by and she adds, as politely as she can manage, "I'll be needing a different nurse. Would you arrange that please?"

***

As a kid, Valerie doesn't know what she'll become when she grows up, but she's aiming at being a detective…or one of the Mouseketeers—who, in *The Mickey Mouse Club* show's *Adventure* segment, get to be detectives like Nancy Drew.

She's only nine years old. She's thin, with long, light brown hair that tubes down the back of her neck in ringlets. She wears those odd, pointy-cornered cat's-eye glasses that tend to immediately disqualify her—in the eyes of fourth-grade boys—as an object of anyone's young crush. But if one of those boys would look past the glasses—which fourth graders just don't do—they'd notice the beautiful jaw-line, the wide-mouthed smile and features that eventually will grow to resemble the hot actress of the day: Vanessa Redgrave.

But boys don't matter now. With her chores done, Valerie and her best friend, a pretty blonde neighbor, one year younger, Lori Fuller, are free to roam the fields and woods and crayfish-laden streams around their homes, pick flowers, chew on clover, and explore old barns.

These days the two are lost in the world of Nancy Drew, the fictional girl detective. The girls burn through the amateur sleuth's mystery books at nearly one a week. This week it's *The Moonstone Castle Mystery*.

They find that it's not enough to read the stories, or talk about them, or even fantasize about solving cases: they hunger for a real mystery of their own—right now. They need to *become* Nancy Drew. They need to live a mystery.

So in the basement of Lori's house the girls draw a treasure map—replete with obscure references regarding locations and perils. They stain the map with the remains of Lori's parents' morning coffee so that it takes on a sepia tone worthy of old parchment. They ignite filched matches to sear the edges of map. They smear a little ketchup in places (Is it blood? They wonder.) giving it an aura of self-delusional authenticity.

With the map job done, they leave the Fuller house and head for the expansive fields that, in the 1960s make up most of McLean, Virginia. They wade through the tall, tan grasses—nearly as high as their heads—until they come to a derelict structure, once part of a farm. The half-hidden shed's walls of weathered, gray planks with inch-wide gaps, seem to lean and sway like a confab of reeling drunks holding onto each other for support. Moonstone Castle.

The girls slip into the castle. The smells of ancient, fecund molds and must gather around them. They dig a hole beneath the rusted iron wheel of an old tiller, roll up the map and bury it. Mystery created. Now they just have to pretend they weren't the ones who did the burying and then follow clues of their own creation to retrieve the map on another day.

Only there won't be another day. Two days after the map caper, the shed burns to the ground. The girls, certain that they had somehow caused the calamity, never tell another soul about it…What if the map survives? What if…? Mystery created in fact.

"Valerie's a romantic. She would make these characters her own; become them," Lori recalls later.

Later that summer Valerie internalizes another fictional girl—Pollyanna, the title character of the 1960 Disney film.

The girls sit in the balcony of the State Theatre in Falls Church, Virginia as Haley Mills, the British-Disney sweetheart, plays the role that will define the term "optimistic attitude." Throughout the movie, Valerie imagines herself as orphan Pollyanna Whittier, or as Haley Mills (no matter, since it's all the same to her). Right away she foresees playing the character's "Glad Game"—which consists of finding something to be glad about in every situation. Throughout the film, as she and Lori munch their Raisinettes and lose themselves in the story, neither can know that Valerie's future —almost exactly— unfolds itself before their eyes.

They smile as Pollyanna's sunny attitude transforms the dour townspeople into cheerful ones. They giggle when grim Aunt Polly sticks Haley Mills in a dungeon-like attic only to find Haley-Pollyanna rejoicing at the beautiful view. They almost bounce in their seats at each of Pollyanna's "buoyant refusals to be downcast." They frown and furrows build even in their child-brows when an accident hits Pollyanna and she loses the use of her legs. Their eyes water, their noses run as Pollyanna cannot find any glad spin for the situation. Finally they sigh, immeasurably relieved, when ultimately Pollyanna walks again and appreciates life all the more. Heavy stuff for seven- and eight-year-olds.

The movie ends and Lori's mother ushers the girls out of the old theatre and toward the car.

Lori looks at Valerie, "I'm sorry the movie's over."

"But we're glad we saw it, aren't we?" Valerie bubbles.

Five — Gravity

Valerie gets dressed today. Once that happens she'll go to the gym for her first shot at physical therapy—at least that's what the therapist says, but Valerie has her doubts. Her hopes and confidence in the future are unsteady, despite her best Glad Game efforts. Throughout the days, her outlook rises rapidly—then drops even more quickly—like the trajectory of a rocket that ultimately crashes to earth. Despite the hope that the word "rehab" engendered initially, and despite her resolve to view everything in a positive light, she's not ready.

"I don't think I can go today," she tells the therapist. "I can't move anything and my neck really hurts."

But this physical therapist—a stern-looking German woman, nicknamed V-2 by her colleagues after the WWII German missile—isn't buying it. "You must," she says—more by way of command than persuasion. Then, "Your sister's coming with some clothes… See you after you're dressed." V-2 leaves.

The room empties again, except for Valerie and her thoughts. She takes a deep breath and whispers to herself, "You're scared." The sound of the words provokes something like an automatic counter-move. *The Glad Game. Yes, you're scared—that's because you're excited. Rehab. Re-habilitation. Re-abled. This is how you will get better. You* will *get better.*

Valerie's sister, Karen, at 55, is a pretty woman with just-off-the-shoulder, blonde hair. She's slender and stands about 5'1'. A nurse herself, she wears a lovely, white sweater set and heels. She enters the room, along with a hospital aide, cradling a wad of clothing in her arms: a pair of shorts, a plain white t-shirt, tennis shoes and a weird—considering the circumstances—bucket hat, the kind with a short brim encircling an inverted can. Stripes of turquoise, red, yellow, lime green, light blue, dark blue and orange encircle the hat's bucket-like crown. A girl might look cute in it if she wore it to the beach—and were extremely cute to start with—except that she'd never wear it to the beach, since the thing is knitted wool. All things considered, it's a ridiculous accessory.

"What's that?" Valerie says when Karen lifts up the hat.

"A hat, of course."

"Why?" Valerie asks, then laughs a little. "Wait. Is this your big chance to make me look foolish? You've been waiting 30 years for this, right?"

"That's it," Karen admits, going along with the joke. But her smile lags behind the fun. She sighs. "Actually, it's an improvement over what you have going on right now."

"Which is…?"

"They chopped off a bunch of your hair in the back—where they did the surgery. Meanwhile the rest of your hair has grown… Listen, just trust me. It's not a good look."

Valerie silently assimilates the latest blow to her self-image. Then she manages a grin. "I'm just ahead of my time. Lay it on me."

Karen and the aide gently roll Valerie to one side, then the other as they slide on her clothes, socks, shoes and finally the hat. When they finish, Valerie looks like she's just returned from a bender at a reggae concert in the Hamptons.

At this point, two tall, muscular gents in hospital whites enter the room, lift Valerie off the bed and lower her into a wheelchair. The sudden change in posture makes her head spin. The non-specific fear reemerges, but she fights it down.

They wheel her along a hall, around a corner, through another hall. On the way, they pass by a woman crying in a wheelchair. No one stands near her. No one looks her way, much less approaches or comforts her. She just cries alone… Never let anyone see you cry, Valerie notes to herself. Smile. Be positive. If you have to cry, do it alone.

Finally, they push through two swinging doors into what looks like a high school gymnasium. A riot of noise engulfs the place—not echoing basketball dribbles, but just as jarring. A multi-ring circus of men, women and children engage in, what is for them, feats of skill and daring, as their handlers shout, cajole, plead, applaud, and cheer them on. Some support most of their own weight on parallel bars, heroically flinging one hand, then the other, along the rails as they sway forward. Some imitate that move with walker-frames. Some simply work on the use of canes. Others lie on "mat tables" as physical therapists lift, pull and stretch their limbs for them.

Valerie winds up next to a mat table. The four-by-seven foot table stands about two-feet high with a two-inch layer of medium-density foam covered by Naugahyde. Two aides lift her from the wheelchair and place her on her back on the table.

V-2 says, "All right, girl. Let's see what you can do."

Valerie wriggles her nose.

V-2 doesn't laugh. "Can you roll over?"

No. The nose thing is about it.

"Okay. Forget it. Today, we'll stretch your muscles and get some blood flowing. We'll be working here Monday through Friday. Plus some Occupational Therapy."

"Occupational Therapy?"

"That's where we work on everyday skills—eating, dressing, grooming, those kind of things."

"When will I be able to walk again?"

V-2 shrugs. "Couldn't say. It's one day at a time… starting now."

Night. The workout ended hours ago. Valerie lies alone again in her dim room. She wonders if her muscles are sore or not. An untouched dinner tray sits on the nearby table. Again, no one stayed to help her eat. But at least this time a cover conceals the food, muting the earlier cruel, tantalizing effect. At this point she doesn't care about food anymore. She hears rain beating on the window, then thunder. The parted curtains allow for periodic flashes of lightning to burst across the room. She wants to watch the light show directly, but can't turn her head; she peeks out the corner of her eyes.

The next huge explosion of nature's light and sound vibrates the room. The hall lights go out. In the next moment, the sound of footsteps running down the hallway fill the place. Staff and nurses hurrying somewhere, no doubt. Hallway lights flicker and die. A power outage. Voices shout urgently.... She wonders, what if there's a fire? All the more vividly, it comes to her again: she can't run or move. Her heart rate leaps... No escape... Then the lights return. The voices and footsteps fade. The place is silent again.

With no one to talk to, trapped in her own body, with no ability to do anything else, she obsesses on the worst. Hard to deny the facts—she literally can't move to save her life. She thinks about death. It starts with the usual what-do-you-think-happens question, then gets more heavy as she turns inward and starts a dark discourse that goes something like this:

... What's left? What haven't *I lost? Body. Job. House. Independence. Piano. Sign Language... Don't even want to think what else. Stop.... You need strength... All right then. Dig down to the depths of your soul... Right. What's my soul? What's anyone's soul? What does that even mean? Soul: "... seat of feelings or sentiment..." So...consciousness? The mind? The will to live? What if I die here?... Maybe that would be better. Life after death?... Is there such a thing?... For that to happen...the soul would have to be apart from the body. That seems true. Look*

at yourself. Your body's ruined, but you're unchanged. You're the same.... On the other hand, the soul, consciousness anyway, seems dependent on the body, the brain. Get knocked out and it's like you were never there... On the other hand... the miracle, the soul, thought, personality, love... how can you attribute all those just to a mess of tissue? It's hard to imagine the whole thing being for nothing... What if science has it backwards? What if instead of creating the soul, the brain impedes it? So... when the brain is knocked out and one is "unconscious," it's really just the brain beginning to get out of the way. If one wakes, the brain is once again in the way. If I just died, it could be that my brain could move completely out of the way and free my soul—no body to slow me down. Freedom.. ...But how?... Paralyzed from the head down. Can't even kill myself... No, don't go there. Never mind... You just recover from this nightmare. Then you can help others who are in the same jam. I mean, that's what you do— did. Right, counselor?... I swear to God, if I get better, I'll do something to help others. Swear to God... Does God really exists? .... Who cares? I don't. Not right not. I' want to go to sleep and when I wake, find all this was just a bad dream.

These types of dark interior monologues now shape most of her nights and some of her days. Despair versus the Glad Game: an endless battle, up and down.

***

Valerie, her mother, father and the Occupational Therapist, a woman named Beryl, sit around a table upon which rest two buckets and two separate heaps of red beads and blue beads. Valerie, still zipped in the neck-to-waist brace, sits in a wheelchair with a seatbelt to hold her in.

Colonel and Mrs. Glines, in their early 80s, normally show no limitations connected to their years. Both lean and alert, they'd usually pass for ten years younger. Mrs. Glines still has a layer of dark hair resisting encroaching waves of white. She wears a white blouse beneath a white sweater with panels of flowers embroidered down each side. She and her girls possess the same wide-mouthed smile; but those smiles can't be found right now.

Today, Valerie's parents do not appear ten years younger. From time to time Mrs. Glines's lip trembles, her eyes get glassy with the harbingers of tears. Dark circles shade the underside of her eyes. She turns away during her emotional moments, so as not to discourage her daughter.

The Colonel fares little better. Bald, narrow-nosed, chiseled chin, he wears the stoic face of a soldier trying to repress emotions—but that takes energy, a lot of it, and his face shows the strain of the effort. He heaves a sigh and tries to make it seem like a deep breath.

Valerie, like her parents, puts on a brave face. She doesn't want them to be sad or discouraged. She sees their pain clearly, which causes her all the more pain, which forces her to smile all the wider.

Today's particular anguish stems from its Occupational Therapy session.

Beryl has asked Valerie to pick up the red beads and put them in the red bucket; and to do the same with the blues ones. How hard can that be? Valerie thinks. Easy.

Valerie stares at the beads. Mrs. Glines forces a grin, puts on an encouraging expression and gestures toward the piles. The Colonel gives a short, you-can-do-it nod.

But nothing happens. Valerie simply cannot move her arms or hands—not even a finger. Not with *any* amount of encouragement. Not with any amount of incentives—not the least of which would be to ease the pain on her aged parents' faces. The session ends in failure for everyone.

As the days move along, the failures mount. They occur in different venues, but the results are the same. Another day, with Valerie's parents on hand, V-2 has her practice transferring from her wheelchair to a bathtub bench. With virtually no strength in her torso or upper body, Valerie struggles repeatedly to pick up her legs and swing them over

50

the edge of the tub. She drips with sweat and fights back tears. Though she ultimately makes it to the bench and back to the chair, everyone—except perhaps V-2— feels tortured. They never try it again.

Aides wheel Valerie back to her room and lift her into her bed where her father feeds her. She thanks the Colonel for his help, but hates that he has to do it, and hates knowing that her abilities are now less than those of an infant.

A week later, things get even worse. Her family takes her from the hospital on an approved three-hour visit to her parents' house. It's her first time outside the confines of Baylor. It's Easter and they've planned an egg-hunt for Valerie's two-year-old niece, Mary Grace. A ramp has been installed so that Valerie can be wheeled through the house to the backyard.

Valerie watches Mary Grace run around the yard filling her basket with colored eggs. The little girl laughs and squeals with every delighted discovery, then runs to some other likely cache in the endearingly awkward way that the very young have. At first, Valerie smiles at the unabashed pleasure Mary Grace enjoys; it's so good that kids can be ecstatic over such small things. Valerie sighs, remembering her own Easter egg hunts—gone now, because of age, yes; but also because well—

Her family wheels her into the house, to the dinner table, and in short order the feast appears. Ham, lamb, mint and so on. It looks so good. That does it.

She'll have to be hand-fed in front of everyone. She loses it and weeps openly.

Pulled by the gravity of her losses, Valerie's spirits crash to the ground and explode like a spent rocket.

Six — The Ghost

Dropping toward Earth, into the depth: of a canyon, Valerie twists and looks up. Once again, she sees the old woman at the receding cliff ledge above. Again, the woman, the fading reddish hair wrapped in a bun, the modest, puffed-sleeved, calico dress of another century, speaks to her clearly. This time Valerie hears her say, "Vaddie, what are you going to do about this?"

Vivian Lucy Townsend, born in Kansas in 1893, puts the question to her grandchild, Valerie Glines, age 6, in the family's kitchen: "Vaddie, what are you going to do about this?"

The kitchen swirls in the simultaneous aromas of baking bread and cinnamon rolls that the two of them have going. A green cookie jar on the counter holds, as Valerie does, a clutch of pecan sandies. Anywhere Gramma goes, loving scents follow. Even out of the kitchen, the air around her carries traces of her lavender soap—her one luxury—in her wake. She puts bars of it on the girls' pillows so that they can enjoy it too. Gramma, a stick of clove between her lips, stands next to the kitchen table, wooden spoon in hand, pulling it around a full mixing bowl. Valerie, perched on a high stool, peers into the bowl.

The issue facing the girl today has to do with a group of first-grade schoolboys who ambush Valerie and two of her friends and take their lunches. It happens whenever the girls take the most direct route to the cafeteria and pass a blind section near a stairwell.

"I don't know," the girl replies.

Gramma keeps stirring. "Well… seems like there might be all kinds of choices. Surely you can think of one or two."

She never tells Valerie—"Vaddie"— what to do, not like her parents would. Instead, she asks the girl what she thinks. The girl loves her for this one thing above everything else.

"I guess we could take the long way around," Valerie offers.

"Yes, that sounds like one solution."

"But that's a really long way and by the time we get to the cafeteria all the good seats will be gone."

"Clearly that's one of the troubles with the plan. What else might you do?"

Valerie stops to think.

"We could get some other boys to beat them up."

Gramma chokes out a laugh that nearly sends her clove stick flying.

"I see… Yes, sometimes that approach works. Your great-grandfather—my daddy—tried it on occasion: only he had to do it himself."

"He did? What did he do?"

Gramma wipes her hands on her apron and sits on the adjacent stool.

"Not sure if you knew this, but my daddy was not only a rancher, he was the sheriff back in Vici when we lived in Oklahoma. Vici was a ranch town. It looked just like that town you see on tv in *Gunsmoke*—dirt streets, wooden sidewalks, two lines of shops on either side; that was it. Well, one night there was a ruckus outside the saloon and Daddy went to see what was what. Turns out there was some boy, drunk, who had called out another boy and they were standing in the middle of the street about to have a showdown. You know: hands just above their guns. So Daddy walks up to them and asks what's it all about. He can see, by the way the second boy is trembling that that kid doesn't want anything to do with what's about to happen, and that the first kid—the drunk one—is the instigator. So Daddy goes right up to that kid—less than an arm's length away—and says, 'Son, why don't you just head on home.' This was the kid's chance, but he was too drunk to see it. Instead, he says to daddy, 'Maybe you'd like to try me.' Now the thing to know is Daddy was a dead shot and pretty quick too. He tries one more time and says, 'Son, a couple things you should know about being drunk. One is that it ruins your judgment. Two is that it ruins your reflexes. Three is that is ruins your accuracy...A shootout right now would be a bad idea for you.' Well, the boy still doesn't take his chance. He moves one step back—so now they are just slightly more than an arm's length apart—and takes a shooter's stance. Daddy says, 'Don't say I didn't warn you...So let's do it this way: that boy over there will count to three. At three we'll draw.' The kid nods, but now he doesn't look so sure. The other boy starts counting. At 'one' Daddy draws, puts his gun just about *on* the kid's gun and blows away that gun's hammer and handle. I think maybe a little bit of shrapnel might have nicked the kid's finger. The kid screamed and began cussing out daddy, calling him a cheat. Daddy said—very evenly— 'It's not a game, son. Some other lawman would've killed you—and he'd be within his rights.' Then Daddy put him in jail to sober up and made sure he got the finger bandaged."

Valerie's eyes dilate like an astonished cat's. "Really?."

"That's what they say... So the tough approach worked...that time anyway."

Gramma gets up and moves toward the sink where she has a standing pot of warm water. She dips a rag into it and wraps the rag around her hand. "Ah, that's better. Arthur has been acting up today." With the rag on her hand, she resumes her mixing.

"Whose Arthur?"

"That's ar-thritis."

55

"What's ar-thritis?"

"That's a problem some people get where their joints hurt to beat the band."

"It hurts now?

"Oh, my yes."

"But you're mixing with it."

Gramma laughs. "Well, you can't stop doing what needs doing just because of pain. Heck, if we stopped every time there was pain, we'd never get anywhere… You can roll the dough. Come here."

Gramma sets out the dough, gives the girl the rolling pin and gets her started.

"Gramma?"

"Yes?"

"You said it worked—'*that* time anyway.' Did it not work some other times?"

The old woman clears her throat. "Yes, there was a time it didn't work."

"When?"

"You sure you want to hear it?"

Valerie hesitates because she recognizes a tone in Gramma's voice that indicates she should think about it. Curiosity wins. "Yes."

"All right then. Well, one day a religious show pulled into town. They were the kind of folks—street preachers— who handled snakes and said that God protected them from the snake venom because they devoted themselves to Him and that they were sort of go-betweens for the rest of us who needed His help. So on this day, they parked their wagon in the center of town and the preacher pulled a rattler out of a box and held it above his head and at his side and all over, while he invited everyone to come see that evening's sermon which would be under a tent about a mile away. Most of us knew the trick—they'd milk the venom out of the snake right before each show—still, a bite would have to hurt; don't you think? Anyhow, in the middle of this demonstration, a man walked up to the preacher and told him to put that 'G-D'd' snake away because he hated snakes. The preacher wouldn't do it. So the man drew his gun—and here's where there's some difference of opinion—some say he shot at the snake; some say he shot at the preacher. In any case, he missed the snake, of course, but he did hit the preacher's hat. The preacher himself was fine but the bullet continued up through a second-story window behind him. The preacher dropped the snake, which caused everyone to scramble. It wriggled toward a farmer who cut its head off with a shovel. That seemed to satisfy the gunman who holstered his pistol. By this time, Daddy was on the scene. He had a friend with him, a Mr. Jacoby. Mr. Jacoby had a double-barreled shotgun in his hands. Daddy came up to the gunman and said, 'Mister, we don't allow shooting in the middle of town. Now, your shot ended up going into that store window up there and right now we don't know if it hit anyone. So I'm going to ask you to give me your gun and come with me.' The gunman said he wouldn't be giving up his gun nor going anywhere. He put his hand on his gun, like to draw. Now you have to understand that Daddy's friend, Mr. Jacoby, didn't even have to draw; he had that shotgun leveled at the gunman's waist already. Daddy pointed this out to the man. Didn't matter. The gunman pulled his gun and shot Daddy dead right where he stood."

Valerie nearly falls off her stool.

"Your daddy got killed?."

"Yes, he did."

"How old were you?"

"A good bit older than you are now."

"What did you do?"

"Oh, I cried and cried and cried for about a week… Until one day my mother—your great-grandmother—I wish you'd met her— she came up to me and said, 'You gonna cry the rest of your life? There's nothing for it now, Vivian. He's gone. Now we have to do what needs doing, or else die ourselves and I don't think he'd like that.' …So we moved on with our lives. Sometimes you just have to pull up your socks, stop feeling bad for yourself and just keep going."

Valerie doesn't say anything for a time.

"So...what happened to the other man?"

"Oh, Mr. Jacoby cut him in half with that shotgun. Turns out the man was a wanted criminal... Anyway nobody won... So, you see that approach doesn't always work... All right then. So what are you gonna do about those boys?"

Valerie, still shaken by the story, thinks for a long while.

"Let's make something really bad today. Some cookies that taste really aw-ful. We'll put them in my lunch bag. That's what they'll get. See if they want my lunch after that." Both giggle, envisioning the sour faces that the first-grade bandits will display.

"I knew you'd figure something out," Gramma says.

During their many and long times together Gramma teaches Valerie to read, sew, embroider, cook, wash clothes and play the piano and dominoes. Valerie hears all about Gramma's life and the suffering she endured and accepted. Gramma's husband, the father of Valerie's mother, shot himself dead after the stock market crash of 1929. Valerie's mother found him in the garage. The community shunned the family afterward, since the people of their town believed that suicide indicated genetic insanity. Gramma, a school teacher, widowed at 35, raised three children herself— working in a one-room schoolhouse, giving piano lessons, conducting sewing demonstrations for Singer, whatever it took. She never remarried. When times turned really hard, she'd say, "Don't worry, I can always add more water to the soup."

Seven — First Movement

Part of the process for rehab patients at Baylor involves a weekly "team meeting." They convene in a conference room where today, around a huge horseshoe-shaped table sit Valerie's main physician—Dr. C, a nurse, V-2, Beryl, and a case worker. Sometimes members of Valerie's family sit in.

Valerie, in her wheelchair, sits at the open end of the horseshoe with all eyes directed toward her—like someone on trial. Beryl reads the first indictment:

"Valerie has not been able to use her hands to put beads in the buckets. I am electrically stimulating her hands but I don't see any improvement."

Guilty as charged. The electrical stimulation consists of what looks like a remote control device wired to patches that adhere to a patient's skin. Electrical currents are sent to the muscles, forcing them to contract like those of a frog in a high school science class. At the very least, the process helps prevent muscle atrophy caused by disuse. It can also increase blood circulation and, at best, re-educate the muscles. But Valerie's hand muscles don't seem to remember anything.

In one session, Beryl announced that they would be going to the kitchen to cook. Valerie sat in her wheelchair—lower than the counter and thus couldn't reach the stirring spoon even if her hands did work.

The jury in the horseshoe hears all this and frowns.

V-2 testifies: "I am not seeing any improvement in Valerie's muscle strength. We are working on her being able to sit up and hold herself upright in her chair—without much success."

In fact, Valerie had begged to try the Standing Frame —a device that looks like a rolling lectern in which a patient, once strapped in, can "stand" upright, aiding with blood flow, strength and the prevention of osteoporosis. V-2 relented and had a physical therapist strap Valerie into one. But the PT cinched the waist binder too high; it rode up, depriving her of the support and the blood pressure help it should give. Having been in either a bed or a wheelchair for so long Valerie couldn't handle the change in blood pressure caused by being upright. She passed out. This failure gets reported also.

Next the nurse: "Valerie has had difficulty holding a fork or spoon even using the velcro strap we put on her hand. She doesn't have the movement yet. She is losing weight and she doesn't drink enough water."

Dr. C: "This week Valerie has not improved with her skin sensations, there is no muscle movement. I don't see any change from previous weeks. I recommend that she gets some pool therapy. I will put in an order for it to start immediately."

The case worker suggests that Valerie have some psychological counseling.

That does it.

"*Counseling?.*" Valerie erupts. "I *am* a damn counselor. And I'll give you all some free counseling right now. You don't create positive results through negative feedback—and that's all I'm getting at these stupid 'team meetings.' You know what might have been helpful?.... If I could have talked to one person who had been through this situation themselves. I asked for that and never got it... Losing weight. Yeah, I'm losing weight and getting weaker too—because I can't use my hands and no one helps me eat. And, hey, I did go back to the standing frame—and once you got the belt on right, I did fine. And by the way, it's a fabulous feeling to be upright, like I'm standing again. It does get my blood flowing... I hear you report nothing but my failures—never anything about my steps forward; small though they may be. But I'm trying damn hard. I'm a dancer. I used to practice 12 hours a day. You ask me for 10, I give you 20. I'm doing what needs doing and I won't stop. ... Why don't you all do the same?"

None of the 'team' responds. The case worker makes notes. *Rebellious. Anger. Denial. Should see counselor.*

Right. Valerie The Demure, the soft-spoken Pollyanna; the deep-running, still water, isn't taking any more of the dark, ruinous bile that comes from her "Team."

***

Her boyfriend comes to Dallas from Denver in the middle of her second month at Baylor. He couldn't be directly faulted for the delay; Valerie had put him off, not wanting him to see her helpless. Finally, she allowed this visit.

He enters the room cautiously, looking around as if something might jump out at him. He gets next to the bed and says, "Hi." He doesn't look at her with a steady gaze; his eyes flit around the room as though it would be rude to look at her for too long.

They exchange awkward small talk. She tells him of her progress and failures.

"You gotta try harder," he says.

She bites her tongue. He doesn't stay long. Something about needing to move his rental car before they tow it. He'll be back tomorrow he says. Get your rest.

The next day he returns—just a little before he's scheduled to catch a plane back to Denver. He doesn't sit down.

"When does your cab get here?" Valerie asks.

"Soon. Soon. Five minutes maybe."

"Well that was quick."

He clears his throat and says, "Val, I don't want to be with someone who can't hike, bike, and do things with me. I don't want to be with a woman who's in a wheelchair. I am going to back to Denver and I wish you luck on your recovery." Then he turns and walks out. Just like that.

Valerie cannot find any words. She feels pain all right, but now she faces the shock of admitting what she's known for a long while… this…this hits hard. The old tapes play again: the "You'll Never Be Loved" insecurity blues move in despite her best efforts. Added to those ghosts are new tapes that sing, "You're Not Even Worth Being Around Now"and "You're Damaged Beyond Repair." She cries for a long while.

Eventually she hears a different voice, the voice of someone she's never met. The *Great* Gramma. "You gonna cry the rest of your life? There's nothing for it now, Valerie. He's gone. Now you have to do what needs doing, or else die yourself."

She stops crying. To hell with him. Just to hell with him.

Pride, in the form of vanity, retards Valerie's progress. She declines offers of visits from her friends—just as she had with her now ex-boyfriend—because she doesn't want anyone to see her this way. She's unaware that visits are exactly what she needs. She needs external morale boosts, especially in light of the relentless assaults on her psyche by her nay-saying therapists. It may be all well and good to pull up your socks and rally your internal strengths, but the truth is, you cannot succeed alone.

With assistance, she can take phone calls, of course, and that helps. She also receives cards, letters, plants, flowers, and gifts from a network of friends that extends all over the country and stretches back to playmates in elementary school. It helps that over the years Valerie has stayed in touch with almost everyone. But perhaps the biggest stroke of luck is that Valerie's friends rarely take no for an answer.

In early May, Valerie sits in a wheelchair in her room, looking out the window at clouds and thinking about Joni

Mitchell's song that describes the various illusory ways one can view clouds, or anything for that matter. At the moment, she's considering clouds' dark side:

But now they only block the sun
They rain and snow on everyone
So many things I would have done
But clouds got in my way

That's how bored and down she gets on weekends when there's no physical therapy.

An aide enters the room.

"You have visitors. They're in the gym."

Without another word, the aide moves behind Valerie's wheelchair, disengages the brake and rolls her out the door.

"You must be mistaken. I'm not expecting anyone," Valerie tells the aide, who does not reply.

They roll into the gym. Lori Fuller, her Nancy-Drew-Shack-Burning-Pollyanna best friend from elementary school in Virginia, rises from a folding chair. Her smile broadens; her eyes gleam with affection. With her stand her lawyer husband —who happens to be another Virginia classmate—Roy Payne, and their two young sons. They've driven from Louisiana, dropped off a daughter at college in Austin, and continued up to Dallas to see Valerie.

For a moment Valerie cannot speak, but she doesn't have to. Lori strides over to her, hugs her tightly, and places her lips next to Valerie's ear.

"Now tell me one good thing about your predicament," Lori whispers in the kindly, frank, joking way that only a dear friend can manage.

Valerie pulls back a bit, looks into Lori's blue eyes, and takes a moment.

Finally she says, "Getting to see you?" The two friends smile warmly at each other and laugh a little.

"How did you know?" Valerie asks.

"Mariel told me where they'd taken you."

So she hadn't dreamed it. It was Mariel Fuller, the nurse back in Flagstaff who spoke to her... Providence or just coincidence?

"God, it's good to see you."

Roy steps up and hugs Valerie.

Valerie smiles. "You're still so handsome."

He smiles back. "Look, I know you two want to talk... I understand there's a pool table in this place. How about I take the guys on an expedition to find it?"

Roy and the kids leave Valerie and Lori alone.

"I want you to know one thing," Lori says.

"Okay..."

"You are going to walk again."

Valerie smiles a little, but then looks down.

"My doctors here warn me about 'false hope.'"

Lori huffs. "There's no such thing," she declares.

Though the visit by Lori and Roy is just an afternoon, Valerie feels somehow physically better. She decides to drop the restrictions on visits.

Valerie's brother, now an officer in the Army, flies to Dallas to see his sister.

Valerie sees him arrive as she's looking out the window of the therapy gym. It's such a good sight that she feels like a puppy seeing her owners return home after too many hours away; she wants to run and hug him.

In a few minutes he appears in the gym. He wears civvies, but he walks with a decidedly upright, military, marching gait. But the rigidity disappears the moment he sees Valerie. He runs across the room to her wheelchair, slides to his knees and hugs her tightly.

She cries and laughs at the same time. "David. It is sooooo good to see you..... I've gotten myself into quite a pickle."

"Seems so. But you look good."

Valerie laughs. She knows that's not true, but it feels good to hear it nonetheless.

She grins. "You know, if I could just move one finger…"

They both look at her limp hands and sigh.

Valerie starts to turn away from that sight. Then her right index finger moves.

Eight — Second Movement

For the next three days Valerie does little but stare at her finger and will it to move. Caught up in the novelty of its motion, Valerie puts the digit through its paces. With her palm facing her, she makes her finger curl towards her: a come-hither gesture. Then she rolls her arm so that it faces downward and turns the finger-motion into that of a scratch. Then she rotates the finger in tiny circles as if dialing a miniature rotary phone. Then she flexes it in and out like the leg of a can-can dancer. She straightens it: a diving board, or an accusation. It can do, and it can be, so many things.

Some of the staff, visitors and patients passing by her door look in and pause at the sight of the mesmerized woman who grins like a lunatic at her own hand. But Valerie hardly notices them and doesn't care what they might think. She senses that this motion opens the door to full mobility and nothing supersedes that thrill.

On the fourth day, Jackie, a nurse's aide, wheels Valerie into the shower room and seats her on the slatted teak chair. Jackie turns on the water—just a little to warm it before releasing it full force.

"Heard you got a finger movin'," Jackie says.

Valerie demonstrates its repertoire. "I've named it," Valerie says. "Indy—short for Index...and Independence."

"Good names."

"Indy does all these motions, while the others—my other fingers—watch. Eventually we'll embarrass them all— the other fingers, the hands, the arms, the legs. Then they'll all have to join in." Valerie looks into Jackie's eyes and chuckles at her own theory. "Now, if only I could get a toe to move too."

Jackie looks down at Valerie's feet. When Jackie looks up, Valerie sees all the white around her irises.

"What?" Valerie asks.

Jackie points downward and Valerie's eyes follow.

Valerie's right big toe twitches impatiently.

***

Slowly, parts of Valerie's body begin to thaw. Though her skin doesn't register temperatures yet, it tingles. Little by little—just as she had joked to Jackie—other parts of her start to move as if embarrassed by their previous goldbricking. More toes and fingers join her dance troupe. At night she feels a "twitchy" urge to move her legs—even though they don't respond. She can move her arms well enough to bump the call button with an elbow. Using the same technique, she can hit the tv remote to turn it on or off. She becomes greedy for physical therapy—despite the demoralizing attitudes of V-2 and the others.

The weekends drive her mad with frustration—Baylor offering no physical therapy Saturday or Sunday since the place lacks a weekend PT staff. So weekends mean two days of doing nothing. Except that Valerie decides to train herself.

On Saturday as she sits in her wheelchair with no one around, she wills her arms and hands to grasp the chrome push-rings affixed to the outer portion of the chair's wheels. She heaves and the chair moves forward. She pushes again and it begins to roll easily along the smooth, linoleum-tiled floors. She feels giddy with the new-found freedom. Then she comes to a section of flooring that's obstructed by carpet and that brings the chair to a quick stop. She pushes harder. Now the chair creeps forward only an inch or two with each exertion—like trying to move a full grocery cart through six inches of mud. But she keeps at it: better than doing nothing.

The next weekend, she maneuvers herself to the vacant Occupational Training room where she glides over to the Hand Crank Cycle that sits on a table (imagine an inverted bicycle's pedals). She rotates the crank until sweat covers her. Every little bit helps.

During her second month at Baylor, her shoulders join the party, moving a little more each day. With the help of a Velcro strap she can now hold a fork sufficiently to feed herself, and use a stylus to hit computer keys.

But Valerie looks forward to pool therapy more than anything else. Though she just bobs around, pool therapy offers the weightless illusion of standing, of being vertical, as she leans against the support bars along the pool's walls.

Today, Valerie sits on a submerged bench inside the pool, waiting for her turn on the rails. She views her floating, bobbing legs. They float parallel to each other, like two elongated balloons. Then something strange happens; her right leg drops *downward*, defying buoyancy. Then her left leg does the same. Her right leg rises; then drops again. Her left leg mirrors the right's motion in alternating sequence. Then it dawns on her: the legs aren't bobbing—she's moving them.

***

Valerie starts to hit the pool several times a week and gets to the point at which she can stand in the water without holding the rails. With the help of Paul—the water therapy trainer— and a light buoyancy belt, she walks from one side of the pool to the other. She feels like someone might who, after being condemned to Hell, gets word that her case is being reviewed. She wants to yelp for joy at the potential, at the implications—but she holds the exaltations back in case that might cause the fickle gods to change their minds. Still...

Paul, who speaks with the soft Southern drawl peculiar to North Carolina, tells her, "You should be 'walkin' on the parallel bars in the gym."

Without waiting for a response, Paul puts two fingers in his mouth and lets rip a whistle that pierces the watery echoes of the aqua-room. He waves and V-2, on the other side of the pool, looks over. He beckons her.

"This girl should try the parallel bars," he announces when V-2 gets in range. "She's walkin' that well in water."

"I haven't seen any indication she can do the bars." V-2 replies cooly.

"I have…" He pauses and shrugs. "But hey, she's your responsibility. I'm sure the attending physician doesn't read my reports anyway." Paul smiles innocently and watches V-2 do a slow burn.

V-2 glares at Paul, then ejects an abrupt, razor-like, "*Fine.*" She turns to Valerie. "If you want to try it. You can try it."

A week later, Valerie rolls into the gym and up to the parallel bars. Two aides help her out of the chair and into a standing position. The "binder," a sort of girdle attached to the sides of the apparatus is cinched on—correctly this time. She grasps the bars, straightens and locks her elbows. Then she stops. Her eyes fix on the clock on the opposite wall; on the second hand moving along its sweeping circle. She stays in that position for a… full… three…seconds.

"That's all," Valerie says, her arms trembling. The aides move in and glide her out of the apparatus and back into her chair. Valerie thinks, Good. This is the benchmark.

V-2 puts it another way. "See? You can't do it. I didn't think you could."

That's because you're a mean-spirited, unhappy tyrant, Valerie thinks. I'll love proving you wrong.

***

June 2000. A little over two months at Baylor, Valerie can walk in water, can move a wheelchair, can feed herself after a fashion, can use a computer with the aid of a stylus attached to her hand by Velcro, can move her shoulders and fingers a good bit—none of which she could do when she arrived. Progress—as viewed by most people.

But the Team doesn't think so. Arranged around the usual tribunal horseshoe of chairs in the conference room, and in the presence of Valerie's parents and sister, the Team renders its usual, disappointed (and disappointing) assessment. Valerie has not met the goals the Team set for her. Each of the team members presents disapproving reviews.

But Valerie hears none of it. First of all, she knows that they're all wrong. Second, it doesn't matter: her insurance coverage has run out. The Team's yammering amounts to a mere performance, a prelude to justify them tossing her out.

The reports become just a drone. Valerie doesn't even look at the speakers. Instead she looks down at her hands. She moves her fingers. Slowly. In time to the metronome of the monotonous speakers. She recalls a simple piano exercise from when she used to play. She painstakingly rolls her fingers in an approximation of that drill. She imagines the sounds that her phantom keys create. Then, there it is—she's playing a song. She smiles, remembering the words. She can hear it now in full. It's the boy from high school singing on a 45 rpm record. He sings *Princess of a Fool*.

She stops playing. The music and singing stop. She hears nothing; the sounds of the Team's desultory reviews having long since vanished.

The perfect quiet of her mind fills with just one thought: John Carpenter.

Nine — Solo

He views himself as a nerd, a geek existing at the fringes of Langley High School's Hierarchy of Cool. (Never mind that almost every kid feels this way, given the universal insecurity of Teen Age in which even those recognized by everyone else as being cool have their own tortuous doubts.) But in John Carpenter's case, he's right; he really isn't cool. At least not yet.

Gangly, thin—maybe 120 pounds—he wears those heavy, Buddy Holly, black-framed spectacles which, unfortunately for John, confer no Buddy Holly panache upon him. Even the Weejun loafers, the yellow, button-down shirt that matches his yellow socks—conforming to Langley's unwritten Dress Code of Cool at the time—even those affectations don't help.

He sits in geometry class and is the one student actually focused on Mrs. Howard as she tries to connect with a room full of glazed-eyed kids who continually check the clock, or look out the window toward Georgetown Pike—which leads to D.C. and Gourmet Liquors, a place that sells beer to just about anybody—or hatch schemes to peek up one mini-skirt or another.

"If two angles are complements of congruent angles, then those two angles are congruent," the matronly Mrs. Howard declares, hopeful that maybe this explanation will result in a breakthrough that will trip the proverbial mental light bulbs all at once. Enlightenment.

But no. The eyes are blank. All except John's.

Mrs. Howard sighs. Her shoulders sag. "John? Would you please come up and explain this to them?"

John ambles to the front of the class for the umpteenth time this year and turns to address the vacant faces. "Imagine a pool table," he begins.

***

John grew up the youngest of four children in a military family. His brother, Dick, ten years his senior, went off to military boarding school at age 14 and never lived at home again.

His father, William Milner Carpenter, graduated from the Naval Academy in 1940. By then, Ensign Carpenter had fallen in love with Mary Alice Comer, a nurse. At the time—and unfortunately for the couple—Navy regulations placed a four-year, post-Academy prohibition on marriage. That didn't matter to Ensign Carpenter. Romance trumped regs and he eloped with his love—keeping their union a secret; just as, in the future, his son would also cherish a secret love.

Soon thereafter Ensign Carpenter took his first post—at Pearl Harbor as a gunnery officer on the *USS Oklahoma*. His secret wife managed to get a position as a nurse on base.

On December 6, 1941, Ensign Carpenter traded his onboard shift with another officer so he could take an overnight leave to be with his wife. The next morning, of course, he woke to the sound of Japanese Zeroes bombing the island. The *USS Oklahoma* sank and Ensign Carpenter's replacement died.

Ensign Carpenter will live to raise a family.

***

John Carpenter, son of the naval officer, scuds through the nomadic life of a military brat, moving to a new "home" about once a year—Japan, Virginia, New York,

Massachusetts, etc. As with Valerie, he faces the nearly impossible task of making (much less keeping) friends. His mother forbids him to play sports; pushes him instead toward the piano.

When his father retires from the service, the family puts down roots in northern Virginia in time for John to attend just one school—Langley High—for four years in a row.

John likes math. He likes science. He likes music and especially the piano. He likes sports too—though he doesn't participate in any—something he holds against his mom. He does, however, watch others play. He goes to the Langley Saxons varsity football games and witnesses the team amass a 4-6 record, the best in the school's short history. Such realms —science, music, sports—make sense to him. They have immutable, clear, reliable laws and rules that provide predictable outcomes—not like the chaos, mystery, and anarchy of human relations, especially those of human teenagers, especially those of teenage girls. Sometimes he thinks that things would be so much easier if only girls didn't matter; if only one could take them or leave them alone with equal ease. But, of course, that's not the way of things.

His path toward emotional chaos begins with football —at the Langley High School Homecoming game on an October Friday night in 1969. A large bonfire rockets upward from a teepee of scrap wood on the idle baseball diamond, igniting a pep rally before the game. From there, the students migrate to the stands to see an under-the-lights game that will become one of those rare Saxon victories—a 21-0 jubilation over Oakton.

John, while in the stands, realizes late in the fourth quarter, that he has lost track of the score or even who's ahead. He's been watching one particular cheerleader the whole time and trying to describe her to himself in one perfect word. He tries on several words for size over the course of the contest: angelic, lithe, statuesque, athletic, beautiful...

but no, there's no one word that will do. One thing he knows for sure: she lives in a different league—not his. Right? Nerd. Cheerleader. Doesn't compute. Forget it. Oh yes, here's the word: unattainable. So just forget it.

But he can't.

He sees her in the hallways between classes. He never says anything to her, just furtively checks her out and imagines how things might be with her. Then again: Forget it, man. Forget it. Stay within your class... your caste.

His fixation with this girl mystifies his friend, Jon Chase, the drummer in the school's *de facto* official rock band, *The Incredible Fog*, to whom John mentions his affliction.

"Who says she's out of your league?" Chase demands.

"I do... and isn't it obvious?"

"No. You need a better attitude about this—or else just move on."

"I wish."

"Okay... Then, what is it about her, huh? She's not the only girl in this school. You've dated one or two. Shoot, she's not the only cheerleader even. Hell, she's not even the only pretty cheerleader."

John just shakes his head. "I don't know."

His obsession mystifies him as much as it does his friend. More strange: at this point, he doesn't even know that he and Valerie have numerous things in common— a military upbringing, playing piano, loving music, performing, being personally shy, socially awkward, and all that goes with that, to name a few. He doesn't know that, after the football games, when the cheer squad goes off to party with the guys, Valerie goes home. He knows only that he actually trembles when she passes by and that no known, reliable theorems explain any of this. So file under "mystery"... which isn't that far from "misery."

***

John has a free period, a shop class that doesn't really require his presence—the teacher pretty much just mailing it in. So he slides out of it every afternoon, goes to the reliably vacant auditorium, sits at the beautiful grand piano there and sketches around, composing whatever comes to him. Today, he works on a brooding piece, which moves along easily—until, out of nowhere, Valerie Glines trots up. He stops playing immediately, then realizes, too late, it would have been much cooler to have just kept on playing and maybe given her just a small smile and a nod. But shoot—Valerie Glines just appeared.—how could he possibly be cool—he's not cool to start with.

Valerie says, "Hi."

He has actually dreamed of such a scenario and entertains some doubt as to whether or not he's dreaming this right now—this could never happen to me. For a brief moment, a low-voltage shock of terror runs through him.

But she smiles and says, "Don't stop."

His face reddens. "I'm just… it's not like I'm supposed to be here… This is just a really good piano…I can come back later."

"No. No, stay. I'm not exactly supposed to be here either. Just thought I'd practice my dance thing. I'm in the musical…Shoot, I can dance and you can just go on playing. It's beautiful."

A brilliant idea occurs to her. "I can dance to your music."

He blushes again and swallows. "I'm John."

"I'm Valerie."

"I know."

They both have the same free period in the afternoons and so "accidentally" meet regularly in the auditorium, during which time, John—heart pounding hard all through it—plays piano while Valerie dances to his music. This leads to some weekend stop-overs at each other's homes—always while the parents are present—each time, music being the overt purpose of the visits. There's no making-out.

This, to John, is "dating." Though he doesn't fully believe any of it—a stunning cheerleader just can't be into him—nonetheless another part of him crackles with an almost electrical energy as he realizes it really *is* happening.

In school, in public, passing each other in the hallway, they don't stop, linger, coo, or even say hi—much less drape their arms around each other and nuzzle. But John understands and rolls with it.

In his mind, they are adhering to an unwritten rule within the Langley caste system, averting scandal, and, who knows, a possible stoning. Stunning cheerleaders do not hang out with nerds—to acknowledge the opposite might rend a hole in the universe somewhere. Or maybe he's fine with it because the romance feels even hotter this way. He (like his father long ago) now has a secret.

For her part, Valerie believes public displays of affection violate one's own privacy—something that no one, especially not a personally shy, socially inept girl like herself, would ever want to do. So she finds nothing strange in the way they ignore each other in the halls. Besides, nothing has happened, she protests to herself—though the part of her that speaks plainly adds, Not yet.

***

On a cold, January Saturday morning, the Langley seniors who want to go to college, or simply do not want to get drafted and go to Vietnam, jam the school's lobby waiting to be herded into the cafeteria to take the Scholastic Aptitude Test which will determine their fates. Because of the egalitarian nature of a mob, John can sidle up to Valerie in a casual, non-scandalous way, which he does.

He smiles and pulls a sheet of paper from his coat.

"Whenever I hear this song, I think of you," he says and hands her the paper.

She unfolds the sheet and reads the lyrics to The Beatles' *Something*. The dancer in her loves the line: "Something in the way she moves attracts me like no other lover."

There he's said it, sort of.

A bell rings. The students suddenly move as one body toward the cafeteria to meet their various futures.

***

Not long after the test, John's heart races, his hands tremble. He and Valerie Glines, fully clothed, stand, face to face, body to body, alone in his room. His parents and siblings are gone and won't be home for hours. He and Valerie came here for one reason: to "make out"—meaning simply to kiss—and only that—just kiss. And kiss they do. One wonderful kiss.

For anyone who has had, and can remember, The Kiss —the one that makes your head spin, heart pound, limbs quiver, turns the world a different color, makes the clouds reverse direction, all that and more—just think about that kiss. It really can't be described or explained, so let's leave it at that and just say that after The Kiss, John Carpenter soars within another world.

This New World cannot be contained or endured in silence. John has discovered something earth-shattering. He must share this breakthrough. He tells a friend about it.

Mistake One.

Mistake Two happens concurrently when he, who is not fluent in the teen lexicon of love, doesn't say that he and Valerie were "making out," but instead says they were "making love."

In short order, this private conversation becomes communal news. Everyone talks about it. It even reaches the ears of a former boyfriend of Valerie's, now graduated, but back in town.

The once-boyfriend, dark-haired, handsome, strong eyebrows and a thick neck, played football at Langley the year before. Though he and Valerie broke up long ago, he still feels a duty of some sort to defend her reputation. He returns to Langley and waits for John in a hallway.

John, for his part, has no idea what awaits; he doesn't even know this guy. John steps out of his class and runs smack into a mob. The former boyfriend, flanked by a gang of students eager for front row seats to a fight, blocks his way and outweighs John by 50 pounds.

"You John Carpenter?"

"Yes."

"Let's talk."

He herds John into the Boys Bathroom. The mob packs in behind.

"What's this I hear about you doing Valerie?"

"Huh?"

"You been saying you did it with Valerie?"

"*It?*"

"Sex. Did you say you had sex with her?"

John almost loses his power of speech—not so much because of the threat of imminent violence, but because of the charge itself. But he recovers quickly. John, for all his nerdity, has been around the planet after all, changed schools a dozen times, and has learned the art of negotiation.

"No to both. I didn't say I had sex with her and, in fact, I haven't had sex with her."

"You didn't you say you 'made love' to Valerie?"

Oh damn. In fact, that's exactly what he said.

"Um... what do you mean by 'made love.'"

"What do you think?"

John pauses and considers his options. One course might be a quick elbow into the guy's eye socket, followed by an equally quick retreat. He chooses a better move.

"Well, if I said, 'made love' that's not what I meant and I fully recant any such meaning if anyone has taken it that way. This is all just a product of my ignorance of terminology. So I'll state now and for the record—for everyone here to witness—that I definitely did not 'make love' to Valerie and I apologize for any misunderstanding that may have arisen from my poor choice of words."

The air goes out of the protector's indignation. It really wouldn't do to pound John now. The mob, disappointed, files out of the bathroom along with Valerie's would-be champion.

But the real fireworks await.

John runs down the hallway to the student counselor's office where Valerie volunteers at that time of day. When he gets to the office and sees Valerie, he starts to explain, but only gets a couple of words out before she screams at him. He can't get a word in, so he yells, trying to get through by sheer volume. The din rises, getting unbelievably ugly. The last thing he remembers is that, in his frustration, he pulls out a penny and hurls it across the room before storming out.

The whole thing, the unlikely dream-come-true, The Kiss, the improbable early find of one's True Love, is all over and done with, start-to-finish, in just two months. Gone just like that.

***

Not long after the breakup, John actually does become Cool. Jon Chase, tells him that *The Incredible Fog* wants him to play keyboards in the band. Now he's a rock star of sorts. Now the Buddy Holly glasses work, conferring all the geeky hipsterism of the Great One. Now those who once shunned him say hi in the halls. Now it doesn't really matter.

John goes off to Roanoke College the following fall and drops out the same year. In the meantime he writes

Princess of a Fool which *The Incredible Fog*—by then in Nashville—record.

***

More than thirty years after The Breakup, John, now national sales manager for an Arizona tech company, makes ready to leave his rented apartment in Phoenix for an appointment in St. Louis. Evidence of his tattered, 18-year marriage lie all around him: pictures of his three daughters when they were young, unopened letters from his wife, who remains behind—with the girls—in their Georgia home, his wedding ring sitting on the dresser. He travels three weeks a month; sees his family on the off-week. Whatever. He misses his children, but not the wife. They never enjoyed a real connection—though a lot of that is his fault. He married her because, when you pass 30, you get married and start having kids—part of a social formula laid out by others. On reflection, he admits to himself that he never loved her and, due to his own... whatever you want to call it... stupidity, loneliness, other-directedness, or just plain unfairness, he's gotten what he deserves. What he doesn't articulate, even to himself, is that he's only loved one woman ever.

He has an oldies radio station on for company as he packs his bags. He snaps the suitcase shut just as The Beatles come on. They're singing *Something*. He pauses and listens. After a few verses, he can't help but wonder what the hell Valerie Glines is up to these days.

Ten — Cage Dancer

The second Friday in June 2000, Valerie sits in her wheelchair near Baylor's patient exit ramp, waiting for the van that will take her to yet another place she doesn't want to be —a $200-a-day private home in a Dallas suburb that purportedly cares for the seriously disabled. As much as she won't miss the negativism at Baylor, she *did* make progress there. She walked—albeit in water. She operated a wheelchair. She fed herself—with the aid of the Velcro stylus. Her fingers moved somewhat. Sure, it took a while; but who cares about the pace of progress, as long as one progresses? Now who knows if she'll advance at all?…She sighs. Better the devil you know…

If she had her druthers she'd be headed to her parents' house. They have a perfect place for her situation: a single-level ranch home with a huge lawn and two people—her parents—who care about her. Her folks are willing to build an addition out back just for her. They'd hire help as needed. But sister Karen has pointed out that their aged parents shouldn't have to deal with the stress of caring for Valerie; besides, an acquaintance of hers runs a private nursing home just 30 miles away.

***

Thirty miles away, flies hang on the screen door of a house in a north Dallas suburb, like shoppers waiting for the doors to open for some big Fourth of July sales event. Heat shimmers up from the residential streets outside and gets trapped under the leaves of the thick elms that line the neighborhood. The home's wooden front door stands aside in a vain attempt to promote a cooling cross-ventilation—which might work except that no breeze stirs today. Hard to say exactly what the flies are hoping for: the inside of the home suffers the same heat as the outside and the kitchen offers no ready food. A musty odor leans hard on the home until you might bet that its weight alone could be blamed for the sag in the interior ceilings.

This single-level, three bedroom, tract home, built in the 1950s, looks exactly like its neighbors: red-bricked and roofed with grey, asphalt shingles and thrown up when they couldn't build them fast enough to meet demand. Now no one comes around much.

The living room and kitchen squat in the middle of the house—both indolent and mostly useless—except for the living room's tv set suspended high on a wall and blaring out the Gospel of televangelists, their congregations, and their attendant choirs 24-7—with an incantation that holds the rapt and total attention of the single caregiver on duty who gazes at the show, living under its spell as she kills time.

Two bedrooms and a bath sit on the western side of the house. Another bedroom occupies the east. Each dark room is just about big enough for a hospital bed, a dresser and a nightstand. Each room has a single, slim slit of a window that stretches from ceiling to floor, offering a narrow glimpse of life on the outside. An occupant, squinting like those who must peer through keyholes or through the bars of jail cells, can take in a few leaves, some blades of grass and an occasional bird.

A woman named Lynette lies on a hospital bed in one of the rooms, her eyes fixed steadily upward at nothing. Oxygen tubes, connected to a tank and a respirator bag, hang around her. The bag alternately pulses full, then deflates, and by that rhythm alone can one guess that Lynette still lives. The respirator, which keeps Lynette going, maintains a constant beep-click-beep drone that never stops. Lynette's been like this, in a coma, for seven years following the birth of a child she'll never see.

Lynette, the lone patient in the house, gets scant attention from the regular caregivers who have better things to do as they learn about compassion from the endless succession of television preachers. One could wonder, peering in at her, if, instead of helping her breathe, the respirator really functions to suck the life out of her.

For the next three and a half months, Lynette, the drumbeat of the respirators, and the anti-Satan diatribes of endless and relentless televised preachers, will be Valerie's exclusive companions—mainly because, with one exception, the caregivers here rarely attend to the residents.

Valerie spends her first three days at the home sitting in her cubicle, that is, her room. Once captured, the inmates here learn the real treatment philosophy of the place: any patient's recovery must be accomplished on one's own. Except in the case of Lynette, where hope has been abandoned, the remaining half of the patients—Valerie—must either teach herself how to recover, or not. If she wants to eat, she'd better just learn to get herself to the kitchen and pull something from the fridge. If she wants to bathe, she'd better figure it out. Same with getting dressed. Same with going to the bathroom. If she doesn't have the strength to manage those things, well, too bad. Right. If you can't administer your own catheter and can't move your bowels, you will die. Tough love, says the televangelist.

On her first night, a pain in her leg wakes her up. She calls out toward the living room, toward the tv, for the caregiver-attendant to please bring her a Tylenol. Nothing. She listens closely and can make out, just above the preacher, the sonorous rip of someone snoring.

The next night, Valerie hears the screen door creak open, then whoosh shut. She glances sideways and sees, through the slice of her window, the night-watch caregiver—the one responsible for ensuring that nothing goes wrong with Lynette's respirator—get in a car and leave. Oh damn. Now only Valerie and Lynette occupy the place. Reflexively, she projects various dire what-if scenarios, which get more and more bleak until, after about a half-an-hour, the caregiver's car returns and Valerie sees her get out, holding a McDonald's bag.

As part of the sink-or-swim philosophy of the place, no one brings Valerie food. So early-on, Valerie manages to extract some cold soup from the fridge, but by Sunday night she quits caring about eating altogether and just stays in bed, listening to the constant blare of the tv as it plays along to the beat of the respirators.

Throughout the weekend, the caregiver on duty hunches before the tv, seemingly catatonic herself. She'll be relieved from her 12-hour shift by another caregiver who, remarkably, behaves exactly the same as her colleague. By Sunday night, Valerie starts tapping her fingers to the tv-respirator beat while simultaneously thinking about the caregivers and imagining Bob Dylan's words coming out of the mouth of a tv preacher:

> *If you're looking to get silly*
> *You better go back to from where you came,*
> *Because the cops don't need you,*
> *And, man, they expect the same.*

She mutters, "I crack me up."

On Monday morning, a cheery, middle-aged woman trots into Valerie's cell.

"I'm Louise. You must be Valerie. How y'all doin' today?"

Valerie manages a smile. "I've been better."

Louise laughs. "Well, I guess so."

Louise looks around and, locating no chair, perches sidesaddle on the edge of Valerie's bed.

"Let me guess. No one has looked in on you and you've had to listen to Pat Robertson and his band of prophets yell at you nonstop for the last three days."

"Pretty much. I hope that's not part of the therapy."

"Har. I think I'm gonna like you, girl. A sense of humor is going to help around this place... Now, hang on a sec."

Louise steps out and Valerie listens to her footsteps clip into the living room. She hears a click and a newscaster's voice chops off the preacher's rant, followed by a shout from the now-off-duty caregiver. Valerie hears Louise take a firm tone: "You hush. You've seen enough of this stuff and 'sides, it's time for you to skedaddle."

Louise reappears, a devilish grin on her face. "I shoulda asked you what you wanted to see before I did that... Is there anything you like to watch."

"I'm embarrassed to admit it, but... I like *Days of Our Lives*."

"No lie. That's my favorite too. Let me catch you up."

Turns out that Louise Hennig, who comes in Monday through Thursday, actually *does* give care to the patients at this home. She attends to Lynette, changing her clothes and bedding, making sure the woman never lies in her own filth. She sits for a time and speaks to the comatose woman—who actually isn't comatose after all. Whenever Louise enters the room, Lynette tracks her with her eyes and, when Louise sits nearby, Lynette will reach over and take the caregiver's hand. To everyone else, Lynette lies stiff as the dead.

Louise, in direct contravention of house rules, makes and serves Valerie's breakfast and lunch, and assists her with bathing until she's strong enough to do more herself. In her free time, about three or four times a day, Louise sits and talks with Valerie over cups of coffee. Every time they talk, Louise massages Valerie's hands with lotion to keep them supple and stimulated. Louise tells Valerie about her joyful, recent wedding in Las Vegas to Richard, the most pleasant man you will ever hope to see, who wakes her up every morning saying, "Hello, Beautiful." and who never says anything grouchy.

As the days of their lives pass together, Louise and Valerie become actual friends; Louise starts dropping by on her days off. On one of those days, Louise leans toward Valerie and speaks in a conspiratorial whisper, "What say you and me go out and about?"

"What are you talking about?"

"Well, you know, go to the mall, that type of thing."

"Right."

"I mean it."

A surge of excitement—or is it fear?—zips through Valerie. She pauses a while before saying, "Okay."

Louise skips around to the back of Valerie's wheelchair and glides her out of the room.

"Where'd you think you're going?"

The on-duty caregiver, seeing the two heading for the front door, has moved her head from the tv to challenge Louise.

"Whadda think you're doin'?" the woman repeats

"We thought we'd go to the mall," Louise declares.

"Who said you could?"

"Well, Valerie, right here, said we could."

"Nnh, unh. You can't take her outta here."

Louise puts on a worried look. "Really? You mean it's impossible?"

"That's right."

Louise suddenly brightens. "Well okay, then…. In that case, you have nothing to worry about." And with that she continues to wheel Valerie through the room and out the door.

After three months of a life confined to the walls of healthcare institutions, a shopping mall looks to Valerie like the wilds of the Rockies. The place has no structure, no regulations, no rules, no schedules, no colored directional lines on the floors. Here people move in random patterns, chaos rules. Who knew that a trip to Kohl's department store had so much akin with a wildlife safari?

"How about you do the rolling from here out?" Louise says as they stop near a directory sign. "This is good practice for you. In here you can practice avoiding people. When we go back out, you can get practice getting around on grass, parking lots with pebbles, around curbs—that kind of stuff."

Valerie nods okay.

Louise continues. "Good. So right now, let's us find the lingerie section of Kohl's, because what you need is a good girdle."

Before Valerie can utter a rebuttal, Louise says, "We'll get you one that's stout and goes to your knees. It'll straighten you up and help you do things when you start walking around."

Walking around?

They find, select and buy the unusual garment, then head over to a Chinese restaurant for lunch. While Kohl's and Kung Pao might seem pedestrian to others, the afternoon for Valerie might be more akin to visiting Disneyland on psychedelics. She feels deliriously over-stimulated—and likes it. She sees an amusing similarity between Louise and R.P. McMurphy, the rebellious inmate from *One Flew Over the Cuckoo's Nest*, who takes the whole company of loonies on a fishing trip.

"After this, you're coming to my house," Louise announces.

"Today? This same day?"

"Sure. I want you to meet Richard and get back inside a normal house for a change." Louise chuckles. "I wonder how many rules that'll break back at The Home."

Leaving the mall, Valerie again rolls her wheelchair through the video game that is the modern shopping mall. After negotiating the cliffs of curbs and real perils of the parking lot, she and Louise drive to the Hennigs' home not that far away. The house sits at the edge of a shimmering lake, a welcoming sight, made all the more welcoming by a tall, lanky, good-looking grey-haired man who beams a big smile at them as they pull in.

Richard, Louise's new husband, helps Valerie from the car, takes her inside and parks her in the living room, near his own easy chair; but he doesn't sit down himself.

"What can I get you?" he asks.

"Nothing. I'm fine," Valerie says, unused to being asked that.

"Well, how about I make us all some screwdrivers?" He looks toward Louise for permission.

"I suppose it wouldn't kill anybody," she allows.

"All right, then," he says and heads toward the kitchen. Valerie can't help but notice that he limps. The two women sit quietly for a while until Valerie breaks the silence.

"Is he okay?" she whispers to Louise.

Louise smiles. "Oh my, yes," she says. "He's fine. A while back though, maybe not so much. Somebody crashed into him while he was stopped at a stop sign."

"When was that?"

Before Louise can answer, Richard steps back into the room, carrying a tray and three, sweating glasses of spiked orange juice. "Y'all talkin' about me?" he grins.

"Yeah. I was just about to tell Valerie about your accident."

"Oh, shoot, don't bother about all that." He sets the tray down and sets the cocktails, with straws, next to the women.

"Go on," Louise urges. But Richard just raises a glass and says, "Cheers."

"My darlin' can be a little too self-effacing sometimes," Louise confides aloud to Valerie. "Okay, I'll tell the important parts… It was a bad accident. They told him he'd never walk again. He was in a wheelchair for four years… Now he takes me dancin'." She smiles ear to ear. "Ain't he sumpin'?"

Valerie smiles even wider at such prospects. "Oh, *yeah*. He's really sumpin.'"

At Valerie's request, her parents arrange for an occupational therapist and a physical therapist to come in and work with her. The occupational therapist visits twice a week, focusing on her hands.

They resume the bucket drill—the one Valerie had failed so miserably at Baylor. Now, however, she's moving the beads into the buckets and even working with hand weights. They work at uncurling her fingers, from a fist, against resistance. For homework, Valerie squeezes putty. Her hand-strength grows steadily.

The physical therapist visits just once, but proves useful in spite of herself.

"I want to try to stand up," Valerie tells her.

"You can't stand."

"I want to try. You never know what you can do until you try it. Come on. Please."

The PT heaves a weary sigh. "All right…roll over to the kitchen sink. We'll use it for support."

Valerie rolls to the sink, grabs it and, with assistance, pulls and presses herself upright. She locks her elbows. The room starts a slow spin, but she stays with it. A full minute passes before Valerie says, "Enough."

She eases back into the wheelchair and catches her breath. When the room slows to a stop, she speaks again. "I'd like to get a standing frame in here. Would you order one for me please?"

The PT nods then says, "If you ever want to walk, you're going to need to see Patricia Winchester at a place called the Gait Lab."

While waiting for the standing frame to arrive, Valerie gets a different surprise: another elementary school friend from Virginia, Annie Hansborough, pops her head through the doorway.

"You didn't sound so hot when we talked last time, so I thought I'd drop in," Annie says, having just traversed a thousand-odd miles so she could stop by. "Here. I brought you a boom-box. Now you can blast the shit out of those holy rollers if you want to."

Annie, in her early fifties, wears a multi-colored kaftan outfit that befits her lifelong bohemian style. The two met in the Churchill Road Elementary School after-school dance classes, now nearly a half-century in the past.

Back then, as now, Annie, the elder by two years, instigated adventures that Valerie, whom she viewed as "charmingly naive," would never have attempted otherwise. For instance, during high school—though this seems tame now—she coaxed Valerie into her mother's car and drove the two of them through the local McDonald's. Mind you, at the time McDonald's occupied the center of high school society. Kids went there to see, be seen, and undertake all manner of plans and negotiations, not all of them parentally-approved, not all of them even legal. Which is not to say that cruising the place's circular parking lot automatically meant ill intent... but it did have that cachet.

On their first cruise, Annie's older brother Wade, happened to be parked at Mac's in his black '65 Corvette. "Duck." Annie commanded—as if that would help hide their identities, as if Wade would not recognizes his mother's car.

But they ducked anyway. Valerie began laughing uncontrollably at this new, big thrill.

"Yeah, looking back it was no big deal," Annie recalls. "But it was at the time and the thing is—Valerie was into it. She may have been sheltered, but she had a taste for trying things."

They signed up for dance classes across the river in D.C. To get there, they took a bus, not even knowing the studio's exact location. They flew by the seats of their pants, practiced together, danced together and afterward never ever lost touch with each other.

So Annie shows up in Texas with a boom box and stands for a moment looking at her gaunt friend. "Is there any chance you can recuperate from all this?" she asks, straight up.

"Could be."

"Well, you're a dancer. You know your body. You know how it signals to you. You have to think about what you have to do to move that muscle. Go from the top of your head all the way down... You just have to reconnect that again. Grace and Dignity.

"I will."

There's a long pause as they gaze silently at each other. Then:

"Your hair looks like crap."

True. The pre-surgical hair-chop done months ago at the back of Valerie's head still imparts that rat-bite look.

Annie takes in the dim surroundings. "This place is pretty grim. Let's get outta here and get you styled."

With that Annie initiates another mall adventure for Valerie. They get Valerie's hair fixed. They buy clothes. They eat ice cream. They shop.

By evening they are ready for dinner and Annie directs them to a Texas steak house—one of those post-and-timber replica bunkhouse places where the air sizzles with the smokey aroma of meat done perhaps too well.

They order drinks—with straws, since Valerie's hands still curl up and lack the strength to hold a regular glass—and reminisce as they wait for their steaks.

As they talk, Annie assesses her old friend and concludes that, though tired, Valerie is excited by the outing and about what it implies—like there's hope that she may one day get back to her regular life.

When the meat arrives they see they've forgotten to do one thing: tell the server to bring Valerie's piece in pre-cut bite sizes. Annie remembers:

"She looked at me and I looked at her and she said, 'I can't cut that.' She picked up her fork and knife and just kinda looked. I looked at her and there was a tear on her face... Despite her brave face during the day, this is where she knew she couldn't help herself," Annie remembers. "So we just sent it back, got it cut up and that was that.

"Anyway, as we were leaving, we go down this ramp by the restaurant's waiting room. It's packed. Well, there's this tall, handsome man in a cowboy hat, cowboy boots and he sees me pushing Valerie in her wheelchair and he says, 'Can I take care of that for you?' I say, 'We're just going out to the car.' He says, 'I can help. I've got 40 minutes here to wait.' So he gets behind the chair, starts pushing and talking to Valerie. He says, 'Where you from little lady?' She says, 'Denver.' 'Well, you're a long way from home. When you getting back there?' 'I don't know.'"

They get to the car and the cowboy opens the door. Annie says, "I can do the transfer."

But the cowboy says, "No. I'll just pick this little lady up and put her right in the car." Which he does.

After they thank him and he heads back to the restaurant, the two women sit in the car and start to giggle.

"What was *that*?." Valerie gasps.

"He was totally hitting on you." Annie laughs.

"No way."

"Oh, yes."

No matter. For a while, life resumes its appeal.

Slowly, Valerie's strength improves. Bathing and dressing remain difficult. An electric toothbrush makes it possible to hold a brush and clean her teeth by herself. But pushing the wheelchair through the house strains her shoulders so much that she has to stop. Who would think that a house like this, supposedly designed for the severely injured, has thick carpeting that impedes the progress of wheelchairs? She buys an electric wheelchair.

When the standing frame arrives, Valerie maneuvers into it every day and "stands" for 30 minutes, enjoying the sensation of being fully upright and being able to look anyone in the eyes who dares to meet hers. Few caregivers will do so.

Meanwhile, the facility's owner reprimands Louise for the unauthorized excursion to the mall earlier—even though, on Louise's watch, Valerie has gained considerable ground. "Valerie got so much better than anyone ever knew." Louise remembers. "They didn't even know she could walk a little with a walker if she just had some braces.

"Yeah, they told me if I took her out again, they'd fire me… I took her anyway," Louise says. "I didn't care about their rules… I think the only reason they didn't fire me then and there was that I gave them notice."

Two months after Louise leaves, Lynette dies.

About that time, an attendant, impatient with Valerie's slow movement getting into a vehicle, shoves her in. Now neglect is being joined by abuse.

Valerie sees writing on the wall. This place *does* suck the life out of people—at least, it feels that way to her. She decides: she must get out; she must return to Denver—the last place she felt useful, the last place she helped others—and to accomplish those things, she must be self-sufficient and she must walk.

Eleven — Children of a Lesser God

1991. Denver. Nine years before the accident.

Elmore:

      Valerie sits in a low chair, looking at an eight-year-old boy as he circles the room examining what it offers. He pauses, picks up a red-haired puppet, turns it over in his hands, lays it down again and moves on. He passes by a faux kitchenette with its miniaturized appliances, chairs and tables. As he wanders, he glances at a doll house and at a sandbox. He keeps moving—slowly—past the big, empty cardboard box, the cans of PlayDough, the rubber animals.

      When he sees the anatomically-correct dolls, he quickens his pace and only slows when he has nearly completed a full circle which brings him to the art supplies. There he stops. He lifts a purple crayon from a table—a table lowered to match the height of young children. He sniffs the crayon, puts it back, flips open a tray of finger paints, regards each color.

      He places a hand flat upon a sheet of rough, manila-colored drawing paper—just enough to create a faint rustling sound—then lifts his hand off the page, like a slowly ascending helicopter. He stares passively at the empty paper for a full minute.

      When he glances toward Valerie, she asks, in American Sign Language, "Would you like to draw something, paint something?"

He shakes his head, no, and never makes direct eye contact.

Elmore has been referred by his school teachers to Human Services, Inc., (HSI) a nonprofit umbrella organization that, among many other things, offers Valerie's psychotherapy services to deaf children and adults. Elmore's school has complained about his violent and destructive behavior; his drawings, they say, are "disturbing."

Not much more passes in this session. Very little conversation takes place, with Valerie simply watching and noting what he does, what he looks at, what he touches. Another session is scheduled for later in the week.

At that session, there is some small talk—in Sign— mostly about Elmore's favorite subject (and Valerie's least) math, and also about his favorite tv shows, video games, and movies he's seen. During gaps in the conversation Elmore plays with blocks, stacking them in patterns that please him, then knocking them down and starting again. Once in a while, he'll raise his head and look Valerie in the eyes—briefly.

Valerie's office is just down the hall from the Play Therapy Room in a six-story, brick building that HSI occupies a block from the Governor's Mansion in a converted Victorian section of downtown Denver. Having completed her psychotherapy internship in 1990, Valerie has set up her office with a homey feel—there's an antique roll-top desk, not situated like some edifice separating her from her clients, but put against a corner wall, allowing a physical (and it is hoped) psychological openness between her and her patients. There's a stained glass window, many plants, some continually-brewing cinnamon tea, and assorted chocolates—a non-threatening, relaxing place. All of her patients are deaf; most of them deeply disturbed by various causes, some obvious, some mysterious. At her desk, Valerie reviews the file on Elmore, compiled by his schoolteachers. He has one sibling, a sister, and lives with both parents in a mid- to low-income part of the city. There's a finger-painting in the file, a representation of a black house with no windows and a red door. Thick, black smoke billows from the chimney. A note in an adult's hand reads, "When asked to draw his home." Beyond that lie papers of descriptions of various incidents involving sudden bursts of temper directed mainly at his teachers and other adults.

During Elmore's third session with Valerie, he chooses to play with the doll house. He twists it around to expose the open back side, then meticulously arranges the furniture: a process that takes a good 15 minutes. He stops and admires his work, nodding his head as if to affirm the arrangement's perfection. Then he suddenly lifts the whole house, upends it and slams it on the floor, breaking the roof and sending shards of furniture everywhere. He grabs bits of house and furniture and throws them wildly—all the while screaming hysterically. When he runs to the far wall and beats on it with his fists, Valerie intervenes, giving him a pillow which he punches savagely until exhausted.

When he's finally spent, Valerie asks him what happened there. He looks down and says nothing for the rest of the session.

At the fourth session, he arrives quiet and subdued. This time, he selects paper and markers. He doodles images of dogs and trees.

"Can you draw your family for me," Valerie signs. "Your house? Or your parents? Your sister?" He shakes his head, no.

"How about drawing what you and your family do for fun? Do you go to the park? Do you ski? What about the movies?"

At "movies," he perks up. "I saw *Hook*," he signs. "Peter Pan comes back for his children and Hook gets swallowed by the crocodile. I wish they'd make it a video game."

"What video game are you into these days?"

"Terminator."

"Does your sister play it with you?"

No reply. No more conversation for the rest of the session.

The fifth session is equally quiet, but during the sixth session he becomes uncharacteristically talkative.

"In science class they blew something up," he signs. "It was cool. You put some baking soda and vinegar together, close the lid, shake it and run away." He pauses to laugh. "You run away because the top blows off... I like seeing things explode... One kid's older brother says that if you mix..." He pauses, this time to remember the exact chemicals, which he's clearly tried to commit to memory. He spells them out correctly. "...red phosphorus and potassium chlorate, you can get a really big explosion."

"But you wouldn't want to do that? Not if it would hurt someone, would you?"

He doesn't answer.

In the seventh session he's quiet again. Once again Valerie asks him to draw a picture of his house. Her mouth slackens a bit as she sees him replicate, almost exactly, the drawing from his file: a grim black house with a red door and black smoke coming from the chimney.

"There's so much smoke coming from there," Valerie signs, indicating the chimney.

He looks her directly in the eyes with an intensity that sends a chill up Valerie's neck. His own eyes seem to be on fire themselves. "That's where we burn things," he signs back.

Valerie swallows hard and, though it doesn't matter if she speaks or not, she clears her throat. "What do you burn there?" she asks.

He is silent for several moments, then says. "Animals... after we kill them."

"You kill animals? Why?"

"Satan wants them. They're for him."

Elmore suddenly rants—his signs now slashing the air in rapid combinations. He describes a circle of people dressed

100

in robes, standing around a campfire chanting and drinking blood. He describes what appear to be orgies and sex between adults and children. Elmore's parents are part of a Satanic cult.

When Elmore leaves, Valerie—per the law—calls the police and the child protective services to report a child endangerment situation. Following an investigation, Elmore and his sister are placed with relatives in another state where they continue therapy. The cult is investigated and busted.

It's a triumph for Valerie, an episode that, while still tragic, makes her thankful for what attracted her to sign language and to helping others in the first place.

***

At age 10, Valerie is introduced to the world of sign language by Helen. The world enters Helen through smell and taste, but far more important to her is touch—the meaning of the world comes to her through her hands. Her hands reveal what objects obstruct her path, who sits next to her, the temperature of her food, the type of garment draping her. Later, Helen's hands and those of Anne, her teacher, will lead to a breakthrough in which she first comprehends the concept of w-o-r-d-s—that things have names and that the names correspond to letters formed by her hands. The breakthrough word: w-a-t-e-r.

It is the climatic scene in *The Miracle Worker* in which deaf, mute and blind Helen Keller, after undergoing months of painstaking work with therapist Anne Sullivan, emerges from her black world.

Valerie sits next to her grandmother in a theatre, watching the movie. At around the 85th minute, prior to the water scene, she watches intently as a close-up of Sullivan's hands, signing various letters, fills the screen. The hands dance, magically animated not just with grace, but with meaning. As much as dancing symbolically communicates, sign language literally communicates via its flowing secret code. Young Valerie's mind registers this amazing art and resolves to one day acquire it.

Her opportunity comes years later, in 1976, when she learns of a Master's degree program in dance offered by Goddard College (Vermont) that would allow her to do course-work elsewhere—specifically at Washington, D.C.'s Gallaudet University—the only university tailored for deaf and hard of hearing students. Valerie creates her own MA program: Dance for the Deaf. The only hiccup is the fact that she doesn't know American Sign Language and so must learn on the fly.

Her every free moment is spent memorizing signs and practicing fingerspelling. While driving, especially at stop lights, she finger-spells license plates and road signs. She housesits an idyllic bungalow in a Virginia forest and, during her moments there, in a cozy chair looking out a vast picture window into the woods, she looks up the signs for everything she sees. She learns the language quickly.

Gallaudet already has a dance program, but it is run by a physical education professor who does not know much about dancing. The "Gallaudet Dancers" basically wing it and sign words of songs as they leap around at will. The professor is more than happy to turn it over to Valerie, who is determined to show the students the richness and variety of real dance forms including ballet, modern dance, jazz, ballroom and disco.

She works with the students five days a week, and continually works on her sign language. They put on a spring concert for which Valerie choreographs Elton John's *Your Song* and *I Need You To Turn To*. The dancers, cued by a drumbeat, sign in time to the music as they dance. They develop a beautiful flow with the movements of their bodies. The troupe travels to other states to perform. Valerie acts as interpreter at hotels and train stations.

She branches out and teaches a disco class and ballroom dancing at night to the deaf community outside Gallaudet.

During this time, Valerie learns at least as much from her students as they do from her. She learns about the culture of the deaf; how some deaf people distrust and/or resent "hearies," how some deaf people say they do not hear silence, but liken deafness to what a sighted person "sees" behind their head, how attempts at oral speech are frowned upon by many in the deaf community.

At the end of the program Valerie has more than she bargained for. She is so fluent in ASL that she now has opportunities as an interpreter as well as a dance instructor. She moves to Denver where she interprets for deaf children in public schools. During the following years, she learns that some of those children and their families might benefit from psychological counseling, but that there are no services designed to accommodate them. Conversing with a counselor, after all, requires a degree of trust and a belief that your therapist has some understanding of your situation—not to mention speaks your language. The idea of sharing all one's inner issues not only with one's therapist, but also with a separate interpreter, severely inhibits many patients. So in the late 1980s, Valerie again travels to Gallaudet; this time to attend a conference on counseling.

There she encounters one of her former Gallaudet Dancers, a woman who now has a Ph.D. in social work and remembers Valerie from her early days of instruction. She tells Valerie about a Master's degree program at Gallaudet focusing on psychotherapy for the deaf, and with a scholarship and stipend. It would require three, six-week summer sessions with additional course work and internships done in one's hometown.

Three years later, Valerie is a licensed psychotherapist specializing in helping deaf patients.

At the same time, Paul Fiorino, Director of Ballet Arts Theatre, learns of Valerie through mutual friends at the Center on Deafness. He wants to do a dance in sign language, based on a poem by T.S. Eliot. He shows it to Valerie with a view to having her work with him on the choreography. She can't know it at the time, but the poem will describe advice that will apply to her later. One passage reads:

> *I said to my soul, be still, and wait without hope*
> *For hope would be hope for the wrong thing; wait*
> *without love*
> *For love would be love of the wrong thing; there is yet*
> *faith*
> *But the faith and the love and the hope are all in the*
> *waiting.*
> *Wait without thought, for you are not ready for thought:*
> *So the darkness shall be the light, and the stillness the*
> *dancing.*

The production radiates beauty and represents what should be considered its own art form, in that it blends the motions of sign language with dance and poetry.

In 1996 Fiorino contacts her again and says he will be putting on a Renaissance dance performance called *The Delights of Posilipo* and invites Valerie to dance in it with him, which she does—reigniting her passion for perfomance and leading her to start her own dance troupe which she dubs, "Deafinite Motion."

Here, however, the confluence of her talents creates the potential for disastrous collisions. She counsels deaf people. What if some of her clients join the group? Conflict of interest could arise. Confidentiality issues could be an issue. But she pushes ahead, and miraculously none of her clients answer the ad for deaf dancers. Her troupe doubles from five to ten and includes hearing dancers and even those who do not know sign language. Valerie soon remedies that shortcoming by teaching sign language to those who don't know it.

For years, Valerie, the counselor, is one of the few psychotherapists, fluent in ASL available to deaf people in Colorado. In private practice, she gets contracts with Vocational Rehabilitation, several school districts, and the state of Wyoming.

In over a decade of practice, she will encounter cases in which she saves lives—and some that parallel her own future.

***

Jane:

Jane slowly pushes open the door to Valerie's office. She enters hesitantly, as if fearful that she might be in the wrong place. Her eyes already glisten with tears. Valerie signs to her, "It's all right. Please come in." But the woman shakes her head and says aloud. "I don't know sign language."

Valerie reviews at her appointment book. Valerie says aloud, "Are you... Jane?"

Again Jane shakes her head. Her voice trembles. "I can't hear you and I don't know sign language and I can't read lips." Now she breaks down and sobs. Valerie gets up quickly and guides her to a chair, then sits next to her and picks up a pen and a pad. She writes, "Tell me what's happened."

Jane, at age 30, has suddenly lost her hearing as a result of a freak infection. Overnight, her whole world flipped upside-down. She tried surgery with no success. She lost her job, as it required her to interact with the public. Her friends are helpless.

She cries throughout the entire session as she speaks.

"Now I don't know what to do with my life," she sobs. "Why was this taken from me? I... I loved music...now I'll never…. I can't answer the phone. I can't speak to anyone. My god, how will I ever date again. I—"

Valerie writes. "You've had a great loss. There are stages of grieving for this—just like when one loses a loved one. We need to move through each stage. As we do that, let's focus on what you *can* do, not what you can't."

For the first time, Jane's sobbing abates.

At the following session, Jane declares that learning sign language and becoming part of "the deaf community" is not what she wants. Instead, she hopes to come up with a coping strategy. She will train herself to read lips, to tell people that she can't hear and ask them to look directly at her when they speak. She'll carry paper and pens so people can write down words if needed. She craves meaningful conversation.

After that the two women work on a list, a positive agenda for Jane. One is for her to find a job. For that, they examine her interests and aptitudes. Jane reads *What Color is Your Parachute*. She takes a career test. She looks into ways to attend a community college.

Another agenda item is simply how to enjoy life. She watches tv with closed captioning. She reads. She rides her bike and jogs. Still, she does those things by herself. Loneliness closes in. She wants to play tennis with her friends again.

"So play with them," Valerie both says and writes. "No reason why you can't. I can show you a few signs and you can show them to your friends so you can communicate what you need to during a match." Jane does exactly that and, in the process, revises her attitude on sign language. She resolves to learn ASL and becomes noticeably optimistic.

Her life resumes its forward direction. Ultimately, she goes back to college, completes her degree and discontinues therapy.

***

Mike Ellis, tall, lanky, sits across from Valerie in her office.

"How was your day?"

Valerie attempts a smile.

Mike is Valerie's mentor, supervisor and colleague. He counsels her on various cases and provides periodic career advice; even runs interference for her through the inevitable tangles of bureaucracy that pop up now and then. He says nothing for a while, then prompts her again.

"So what happened today?"

Valerie straightens up and takes a breath. "Well," she begins. "A woman came in today. She was referred to me from Ft. Logan—you know, mental lock-up place? They wanted me to evaluate her. They were letting her out, but they sounded a little hesitant. I should have picked up on that. Anyway, I was sitting in that chair." Valerie points across the room. "This woman was sitting in the chair by the door... I know, I know. Big mistake right there. 'Never, ever get into a position where you can't make a quick exit.' So after just a few words, this gal goes nuts, jumps up and pulls out a huge knife—a Bowie knife, hunting knife, something like that—and puts it to my face."

"She wha—? What'd you do?"

"I remember being really scared but I heard your voice in my head going through the drill: stay calm, don't show emotions. So I faked being calm and signed to her. I was able to talk her into putting the knife away. The moment she put it away, she—not me—ran from the room."

"Lord. Are you all right? You're not going to quit or anything, are you?"

Valerie laughs. "What?... What are you talking about? Quit? No way... I'm the happiest I've ever been in my life."

Throughout the 1990s, Valerie continues her practice and travels the country, giving presentations at national conferences. She works six to seven days a week. She offers a sliding fee scale that goes as low as one dollar per session. She's on call 24/7. She never takes a sick day. Never takes a vacation. She has purpose. She feels alive. She helps others find relief. She exorcises demons. She's never bored. She is a woman in full.

Twelve — A Dancer's Gait

<u>Mid-July 2000</u>.

"Dad. Mom… I've got to get back to where my life had meaning. To do that I've gotta get out of here. To do that, I've gotta be self-sufficient. To do that, I've got to walk."

Valerie's parents and sister huddle around her bed at the nursing home. They listen intently. Nothing would please them more than to see Valerie recover. But sister Karen, a nurse, has seen too many patients crushed by the disappointments that follow false hope. She blurts out, "Valerie you will never walk, so just get over it. Get used to being in a wheelchair and move on."

All the air sucks out of the room. Since sound can't travel in a vacuum, silence prevails. After several agonizing moments, Karen says, "Look, I didn't mean it to sound so—"

Valerie waves off the apology.

"In order for me to walk," she continues. "I need some serious therapy. I found a place called the Gait Disorders Clinic. It specializes in walking. It's affiliated with the UT's Southwestern Medical Center. I've already spoken with a woman named Patricia Winchester. She told me I could come in for an evaluation to see if there's anything they can do for me."

"Oh, darling, that's wonderful," her mother says, clapping her hands together.

"Here's the thing," Valerie goes on. "If I'm admitted, the sessions will be $200 an hour and insurance doesn't cover it."

The newest and best collection of therapeutic equipment, machines, video cameras, glass flooring (to measure steps), astound the Glines family as they enter the Clinic. It reminds Valerie of the elaborate trappings of backstage paraphernalia at the theatres where she's danced.

A petite blonde with frizzy hair and blue, cut-off overalls greets them.

"Hi. I'm Patti. Let me show you around."

She guides the group into what, at first, appears to be a spacious training facility for an Olympic gymnastics team or a NASA space simulation building. Parallel bars of various heights and configurations occupy one corner; free-weights and weight machines are splayed about, but a closer look reveals the floor's specialty. One entire wall is a blue-screen for video captures of patients as they maneuver along a black floor, painted with yellow grid lines, measuring and recording every step. In another part of the room a patient, harnessed like some kind of paratrooper or deep ocean diver, is cantilevered above a treadmill, and takes carefully supervised steps as he supports himself with his arms on parallel rails. Another patient moves within a four-wheeled walker, while an electrical device belted around his waist, sends impulses to his calf muscles, helping him raise the angle of his feet. Sweat pours off his face.

To some, the scene might appear grueling. But Valerie's eyes light up like those of a child on Christmas morning.

"Let's go over to the mat table and see what you can do—see what we have to work with," Patti says, wasting no time.

They move to a low, padded table and transfer Valerie onto it. Patti moves and tests the motion in Valerie's ankles, legs and feet. She asks Valerie to flex her foot. Valerie tries desperately to do so, but the foot doesn't budge. A surge of panic zips through her: what if she's not accepted into the program?

After some time, Patti straightens up and sighs. She and an assistant transfer Valerie back to her wheelchair. She looks Valerie in the eye.

"I think we have enough to start with," she says finally. "You can come twice a week and we'll see what happens."

Valerie squeals in delight. Her mother clasps her hands to her chest and beams. Her father says, "Outstanding."

Patti holds up a hand. "Oh, we're not done today. We start now. Valerie, let's hit the treadmill."

Without further ceremony, Patti and her assistant wheel Valerie to one of the huge treadmill contraptions. They strap her in, placing a parachute-looking harness under her butt, then hit a button that lifts Valerie into a standing position. Standing. Just like that. Just the sensation of being vertical makes Valerie's spirits leap. Another button and the treadmill moves slowly. The two therapists crouch down and move Valerie's feet for her. They continue for five minutes until Valerie loses her breath. A long-gone feeling of hope replaces all the energy that Valerie expends that day.

Valerie works out at the Gait Clinic twice a week, beginning with the harness-treadmill. Each visit feels to her the way a summer NFL training camp might feel to a rookie. Hard work, unrelenting, exhausting, often repetitive and boring—but the only way to get where you want. And each time, she notes incremental increases in her strength, endurance and mobility—enough progress to thrill her, to keep her hungry for more.

She graduates from the treadmill to a harnessed walker, a huge device that actually moves while she takes real steps—all the while the bulk of her weight suspended from an attached, bowed arm above. Weeks of this pass until at last Valerie advances to the point where she can tackle a normal, four-point walker and, leaning against it, support her own weight and take her own steps.

On the days she spends back at the nursing home, Valerie practices moving around the house using the walker. The caregivers, with the exception of Louise, offer no encouragement and instead make shoo-ing waves of their hands if she passes between them and the televangelists on the tube. One evening Valerie's walker catches on the leg of her bed and she, along with her walker, crash to the floor. Reflexively, Valerie calls out for help. No sound. She calls again. Finally Valerie hears the voice of the on-duty caregiver nag at her visiting boyfriend: "Well durn it all, Ruben, be good for somethin'. Go lift that girl up."

On August 13th, 2000, Valerie celebrates her 48th birthday at her parents' Dallas home. She'd received an early present several days before: the news that she would not have to wear her cumbersome, heavy plastic neck brace anymore. But, afraid to remove the gear, she wears the brace anyway, even to her little party. She doesn't tell anyone the news. She decides to surprise her parents and maneuvers her walker to the large bathroom, closes the door, faces the mirror and unbuckles the brace. She stares at the scar that knifes across the front of her neck. She can't help but see a gruesome resemblance between her own neck and that of a slasher's victim. She thinks her neck looks hideous and considers wrapping a scarf around it. *But no, damn it.* (Pollyanna and the Glad Game re-emerge.) *It's my birthday and I'm not going to let this spoil my day. I'm glad to have made it through another year.*

At the end of August, Valerie's rehab regimen moves to crutches—not the type that go under one's armpits, but the kind that appear to clip onto one's forearms. She uses two of them, at first just to toddle around the workout rooms. As her arm-strength and balance improve, she takes on more difficult journeys. By the end of September, she takes her crutches outdoors and takes on uneven surfaces and curbs. She tells her parents that it's time for her to go back to Denver.

Thirteen — Downtime in the Rockies

List for Denver:
— Find apartment.
— Get furniture out of storage.
— Get a job, any job.
— Find physical therapy.
— No, not any job. Counseling.
— Connect with friends.
— Get my cat.
— Get computer.
— ~~Date?~~
— Have someone counsel me.

Moving, under any circumstances, wears one down. But when one is alone and hurt… well, there's just no way to do it without a lot of help. Fortunately for Valerie—and perhaps a tribute to her affect on others—her friends step up.

While in rehab, she'd asked a friend, Tim Wayne, a realtor, to sell her town house. He did, took no commission, and placed her possessions in storage. Karen flew ahead and acquired an apartment for her sister near Valerie's previous home. Friend Ali Ford, despite having two cats of her own, took care of Valerie's cat throughout the six months of rehab; Terrie McAlarney kept all 82 of Valerie's plants alive; Jack Wendt, described as "a jolly old neighbor of 75 years from Nova Scotia" will scrape ice off Valerie's car, warm it up, walk her to it on snowy days, and collect her mail. Becky Taillon will help her on weekends with grocery shopping, errands, and anything else left undone.

So, on October 1, 2000, Valerie flies home to a welcoming and supportive troupe.

Connect with friends: check.

Apartment: check.

Furniture: check.

Cat: check.

Computer: check.

But the weird thing is this life called "normal." That first night. The night when you bed down alone for the first time in six months. When *you* make the decisions. When it's all up to you. There's a rush of freedom, or course—the newness of privacy and optional silence. But before this, "normal" had become a life of fellow patients, hospital beds, nurses, doctors, careless caretakers, televangelists, supervised physical therapy... now she has beamed back into a previous life, a life that doesn't quite fit anymore. Of course nothing has really changed in Denver; it's Valerie who's different. Not unlike a war veteran who returns to his hometown after being stationed in a surreal hell, or like a long-term prisoner finally released who now wonders which life is real and which is an illusion, Valerie feels a bit "out of it."

One night, around three a.m., a booming crash wakes Valerie from a deep sleep. It's the sudden exploding sound of rushing water blasting through the darkness. She scrambles around to find her walker, then struggles to the living room and flicks on the lights: a waterfall pours down from the ceiling. For a moment, panic paralysis seizes her. There's a dreamlike haze still clouding her mind and she's briefly confused as to whether she's dreaming or not—and if not, is she going to drown? She snaps out of it and calls the apartment complex's emergency maintenance number. Turns out that the people above Valerie are not at home and their water heater has broken. Other than damage to Valerie's furniture, artwork and antiques, everything settles down. Except Valerie's peace of mind.

Living independently has a downside. For most of us, everyday activities are nothing more than minor errands, but for someone in Valerie's state, they loom large. For instance, the mail.

There's a community mailbox at the entrance of the complex. To get her mail on the days that someone like Jolly Jack isn't available, Valerie puts a bag around her neck—freeing her hands and arms to operate the crutches—then she maneuvers around the cars and up and down curbs, then balances on the crutches, unlocks the box, removes the mail and transfers it to the bag, all before losing her balance and securing the crutches again. If there's a big package, or if it's snowing, forget about it.

Speaking of snow in Colorado, Valerie will encounter a blizzard. It snows three feet in two days. She can't get out her door. Drifts pile up against the windows. Fortunately, Valerie has enough food stashed away to wait it out—and the power stays on.

Another night, the smoke detector alarm goes off due to a faulty battery. Most of us would haul out a ladder, find the offending detector, replace the battery and grumble back to sleep. Valerie must abide for several days before anyone can come and fix the piercing shriek of the damn thing.

Of course, if Valerie falls while living alone, there could be big problems. So there's that constant anxiety.

Nonetheless, Valerie sees herself on a mission to Normal. Next step, get a job. A counseling job.

By this time—November—Valerie propels herself via two canes, rather than crutches. As luck would have it, she hears of a position as a psychotherapist at—get this—the U.S. Postal Service in Denver.

The phrase "going postal" originated in the media 1993 after a series of incidents from 1986 on in which U.S. Postal workers shot more than 40 people in at least 20 incidents of workplace rage. Valerie's job—contracted through a Chicago-based company—would be to counsel Post Office employees and their families as needed.

She works with both hearing and deaf postal employees—a surprising number of whom have gambling addictions, one of whom, despite making a good salary, lives in his car. Most of the people she sees have typical problems —marital issues, self-esteem issues, etc. No one, fortunately, on the brink.

Before going to work at the Post Office, Valerie undertakes physical therapy sessions at Denver's Craig Hospital, one of the nation's best facilities at treating spinal cord and brain injuries. Per arrangement with her supervisor at work, Valerie can workout at Craig from eight to 10 in the morning, then make up the time at the Post Office at the end of the day.

Craig Hospital's physical therapy unit has it all and, as the years go by, gets more. There are therapeutic cold lasers, neuromuscular electrical stimulators, computerized gait assessment videos; there will be a Locomotor treadmill training system, and a Locomat Robotic-assisted gait training machine. It is the Gait Clinic and then some. The staff is friendly. The atmosphere is casual. The nurses wear jeans if they want.

Valerie ups her regimen to three times per week—a process that will continue for years. Later, when the hospital acquires the Locomat, Valerie is one of the first to try it. She is suspended by a harness above what looks like the hips and legs of a Star Wars Stormtrooper. These white, robotic appendages attach to her own legs and assist Valerie's walking motion while on a treadmill. At the same time, a therapist crouches low to make sure Valerie's left foot does not lazily drag downward on each forward step. There are, of course, plenty of other—less exotic—forms of PT. There's core work on the mat table (crunches), light weight work (curls with small dumbells), and stretches and balancing on one foot. And sweat. Plenty of that.

After each workout, she drives (yes, she drives now) to work where she stays until late at night, filling out post-counseling notes and planning the next day. Some nights, she's the only one left in the building. It's a long walk on a tile floor to the elevator and then a long walk in the dark to her car.

The scariest part is actually the tile floor—slippery in the best of circumstances, treacherous to someone maneuvering with two canes. One fall and she could be on the floor all night. Her most ardent prayer: a non-eventful walk down the hall. (One day the fire alarm goes off. By the time Valerie collects her backpack and leaves her third-floor office, the place is empty. Since, during a fire emergency the elevator doesn't operate, Valerie's alternative is to navigate three flights of stairs—not something she's prepared to do. She stands in the hall and waits, hoping, correctly, that it's just a drill.)

So, at the end of each day, once Safe Passage Prayers are answered, Valerie drives an hour back home. When she arrives, she's often too tired to eat and falls asleep with her clothes on. Life becomes work, physical therapy, sleep.

While administering Valerie's workouts at Craig, a therapist, knowing Valerie's credentials, asks her if she would talk to a patient. She leads Valerie to a young girl's room.

Drapes drawn, darkness owns the room. The darkness seems to make grief visible. As Valerie's eyes adjust, she sees the girl's parents seated in a corner. Medical equipment—IVs, heart monitor, ventilator—surround the girl, who is just 17 years old.

Valerie introduces herself. The parents just nod. Then the mother says, "She refuses to eat."

"I had a hard time with that too," Valerie says. "What happened?"

"Car accident. Her car slid on ice and flipped. She wasn't wearing a seat belt. Broke her neck. She was a cheerleader."

"I was cheerleader once... May I speak with—?"

"Murphy. Sure, speak to her if you want."

Valerie approaches the girl's bedside.

"Hi. I'm Valerie. I broke my neck too. You're probably angry and scared. I know you can't speak right now, but let me tell you a little bit about what I've learned."

Valerie recounts her tale thus far. The girl, immobile, watches her. The only sign that she hears anything is a tear that rolls down her cheek.

In the weeks that follow, Valerie visits regularly and reiterates the same themes each time: look forward, strive to move forward, make the best of life. Privately, Valerie thinks of herself having had 47 good years in a good body and this girl only having had 17. (Many years later, Valerie will discover the girl on Facebook and learn that she completed college and traveled in Europe).

The experience puts an idea into Valerie's head: she's a licensed psychotherapist who can relate not only to the emotional issues of the deaf, but also to people who are mentally traumatized by physical injury. She could work at a hospital like Craig. She files that note for later, as her plate is full for the time being.

As the year turns, the Chicago mental health company loses its contract with the Post Office, spelling an end to Valerie's work there. But she soon finds another job at nearby Littleton High School as its Student Counselor and At-Risk Coordinator, where she helps identify troubled students and coordinates, when needed, intervention plans between them, their parents and educators.

Still, life doesn't change much except now she must rise at 3:30 a.m. be at work by seven. Her physical therapy commences in the late afternoon.

Every month Valerie becomes a little stronger, but she still has very little social life as her time and energy remain divided between work, therapy and sleep. And, despite her innate positive outlook, her Pollyanna heroine, the Glad Game, the help from dedicated friends and her own sheer will, she fights depression daily. Oh yeah, make no mistake: battling back from this kind of injury is not an ongoing, uplifting saga of nobility, heroism and triumph. It's hell every day.

She spends holidays alone—despite being invited to various friends' events. One girlfriend invites Valerie to see the Broadway musical *Annie*. She goes, but deep down regrets it. Instead of uplifting her, the performance reminds her that she can no longer dance and that void fills with despair. So when another friend, with season tickets to the Colorado Ballet, extends an invitation, Valerie declines. She just can't do it. It's not just that; traveling is risky. She has to time her bodily functions just so when she goes out. Besides, the holidays offer her the rare luxury of rest. Even so, it's hard for a sentimental person to see Christmas come and go without festivity.

On the fleeting occasions when she has time and enough energy, she'll sit down and watch television. But even that isn't safe. Movies will sneak up on her, especially the classic movies—Fred and Ginger dancing. She'll watch for a while, admiring the costumes and choreography, but before long she'll be sobbing, thinking that if she could just be "normal" again, all she'd want to do would be dance.

In a place that no one is allowed to see, Valerie questions whether she can keep it together for even one more day—much less the rest of her life. And that question comes up every day. She rates success as a day where she's avoided any kind of accident and is relieved when each day ends.

Life seems to stretch out before her in a way that seems entirely too long.

Fourteen — Transition

Valerie reaches a point of desperation such that, when a colleague suggests she see a New Age "spirit channeler," named "Lightsong," she doesn't entirely dismiss the idea. It's not really her cup of tea and she doesn't believe in channelling or other non-scientific approaches to mental health, but, to be nice, she goes.

She finds Lightsong's house on a large lot at the end of a dead end suburban street; the home densely surrounded by thick bushes and a packed stand of ash trees, such that the house itself blends into the background. A diminutive older woman in a flowing, multicolored skirt and 1960s-era peasant blouse—Lightsong—greets Valerie at the door and ushers her into a living room that features a mantle packed with crystals and an indoor jungle of oversized plants that reach up to the ceiling.

Valerie briefs Lightsong on the terrible events of her life recently. Before Valerie says much more, the woman switches on a tape recorder, closes her eyes and begins to speak in the most soft of voices—ostensibly articulating the hidden words and tone of Valerie's soul.

Some of Lightsong's utterances and insights, occurring over many sessions and edited for clarity, follow here:

I didn't lose myself or body. It is not physical death but still a loss of life. Sadness is a buffer that doesn't allow me to move on. It overshadows everything. It's a deep sadness coming not from this, but from my former life.

Sadness takes my energy and vitality. It blocks my body, my abilities, relationship with myself. Yet I continue to live. Is it a punishment instead of a blessing? Find the answer to that. There is a blockage preventing me from being me again, from receiving myself fully. There is doubt and the belief that I have done something to cause this drama. I reject myself. Forgive myself. That is the first step. Look at myself, embrace myself, accept myself. Opening – self judgment is moving through. I am angry at him, at God, at the world and this anger I turn on myself. I blamed myself because he didn't love me. That is his *failing, not mine.*

Sadness starting to move, heal. Understanding the fall. I did not believe that the goodness in my life was real. I believed it would be taken away. Past experiences, past lives? I have profound experiences of losing what is dear to me. I wanted to touch the darkness and pain of what people have in themselves and find a spark of light. I have seen other people's lives and their suffering – always my purpose to go to the bottom of what is wounded in people – awaken the seed – that which is in the human psyche… Love and the divine can blossom again – suffering can be transcended. I came into human form to touch the darkness of suffering, to have my experience. I leave a trail of light, that others can tap. My life is to serve. My own persona, ego, intellect has to adjust because my soul follows a greater need. My own suffering brought me to a place where I experienced the loss instead of greater good. That will change… My bodily form of my life was shattered, calling me to connect with the force of my own being…. I feel lighter. Sadness is leveling off. This allows me to open up. There's a strength and giftedness I had not touched before. When soul goes into action, it never holds logic like the mind. Soul transcends any level of separation and illusion we hold. I am transcending security-based-on-form. Form changes constantly. Find acceptance and meaning to who I am.

I made a mistake—my pattern of being so hard on myself. I never loved myself truly. Any good I had I didn't think I

deserved, or should keep. I won't prove myself anymore.
Reevaluate relationship with myself. There is a shift. Vitality is
coming back.

I am a beautiful being, so far greater than my body. It
can happen: a rebirth—of love myself for myself and for others...
I can tap into and live my potential far beyond what I have
known. I need to jump start my body. Healing in the spine,
movement and feeling will continue. Distrust of my body because
it failed me, caused me pain and loss. That is changing. Pay
attention to change. I feel it. I will have love in my life again
with someone who will appreciate me for who I am.

Think what you will of channelling, or New Age
hocus-pocus (or psychotherapy for that matter), the proof is
always in the pudding and the words that Lightsong speaks to
Valerie ring true to her—as true as any psychotherapeutic
epiphany...perhaps even more so, given that the final line of
Lightsong's speech becomes prophetic later. In any case,
Valerie receives a second wind.

Fifteen — Pause

On good days in 2002, John Carpenter feels that his life is on hold. On bad days, he feels it slowly sinking toward nothing.

He lives in Massachusetts, running a struggling company called VAM (Value Added Marketing). His wife, Cleaves, lives in Georgia. His youngest daughter, Page, lives with her mother and attends high school. His twin girls, Kristen and Hilary attend college at the University of Georgia and Georgia Southern respectively.

The couple's relationship, stretched to its limits for a long time is about to snap. Surprisingly, the problem is not rooted in John's career which, over the years, has had him— but not the family—located in various parts of the country or has had him travel three out of every four weeks a month. The strain comes from the usual issues that occur whenever a couple picks the wrong partners for the wrong reasons. Eventually something's got to give. And despite attempts at reconciliation and a five-month re-cohabition, both John and Cleaves know their union is doomed.

From the outside looking in—years earlier—the family looks typical—apart from the five dogs and two cats. Cleaves works for a veterinarian. Page and Kristen own their father's musical aptitude. Page plays the clarinet and violin. Kristen, who will become a music major in college, plays the oboe. Hilary, however, is unique within the family.

Born prematurely, and suffering from hydrocephalus, she doesn't walk until she's four years old and, during her formative years requires a great deal of care, as her development is delayed in many ways. John obsessively provides the care needed and then some. It becomes his great transformative event—bringing him from lost soul to dedicated caregiver.

Hydrocephalus is the excessive accumulation of cerebrospinal fluid (CSF) in the brain. Normally, CSF flows through spaces in the brain called ventricles, then exits into reservoirs at the base of the brain. Normally, CSF bathes the surfaces of the brain and spinal cord, and then reabsorbs into the bloodstream. The fluid is vital as a shock absorber, deliverer of nutrients to the brain, remover of waste, and balancer of the amount of blood in the brain.

With hydrocephalus there is an abnormal widening of the ventricles. This widening creates harmful pressure on brain tissues and, if left untreated, can be fatal. Approximately one in 1,000 babies is born with hydrocephalus.

The condition is most often treated by inserting a shunt system—a plastic tube, catheter and valve—that diverts the flow of CSF to another area of the body where it can be absorbed.

The success of shunt treatment varies from person to person, but some people—like Hilary—recover almost completely after treatment and have a good quality of life.

John takes Hilary everywhere. And while parents will say that they love their children equally, that's not always strictly true: they have favorites and Hilary is John's.

But now the nuclear family has exploded. The eldest girls are off to school; the youngest lives 1,000 miles away with John's estranged wife and when they divorce John will appear to be the villain.

He moves into an old mill condo in Lowell, Massachusetts near his old friend and bandmate, Jon Chase. For solace he jams with Jon in Jon's recording studio.

From time to time he thinks back to the last and only time he's seen Valerie Glines since the awkward 1972 music delivery at her dorm doorway in Boston. The vignette takes place in 1990. He spies her across the floor at the Great Falls Grange Hall—the regular reunion site of the Langley High class of 1970. She wears her hair in a puffy perm. Her body is trim and tanned, and encased in a stylish, sleeveless, red jumpsuit. Towering next to her is a bearded giant of a man—perhaps six-foot-five—in a pink polo shirt and grey slacks. He looks like a white, NBA star. No one like that went to Langley; not in their class. John looks, but doesn't approach. He's with Cleaves anyway and doesn't see much good coming from having the two of them meet.

He turns away, guiding Cleaves with him, and is about to skulk off to another part of the hall when a jubilant shout catches him.

"John. John Carpenter."

He turns to see Valerie almost running after him. She catches him and throws her arms around him.

"My God. I was hoping I'd see you here." she bubbles.

Meanwhile, Valerie's giant crosses the floor in a couple of strides. She pulls away from John, remembering her manners, and still smiling ear to ear says, "John, meet my husband, Tim Daniell. Tim this is John Carpenter—he wrote the music to the first dance I ever choreographed."

The men exchange handshakes. John stares. He floats in a momentary stupor, unable to reconcile this enthusiastic reception from Valerie with the inhospitable one he'd received from her almost 20 years earlier. He neglects to introduce Cleaves.

Valerie takes Cleaves' hand. "I'm Valerie. This is my husband Tim."

"Cleaves. John's *wife*."

John recovers and apologizes. "I… I'm just surprised to see you here. What have you been doing?"

A very abbreviated version of updates pass. The couples quickly disengage and drift elsewhere.

"What the hell was *that*?" Cleaves asks as soon as they're out of ear-shot.

John, electing to interpret the question differently than intended, changes the word-emphasis and replies, "Exactly. What the hell *was* that?"

Valerie and John don't get a chance to converse again that weekend.

In 2000, a decade after that reunion, Valerie, now struggling to recover from her spinal cord injury, finds an email address for John and writes to him. He replies immediately, thus:

vdaniell

From:	*John Carpenter*
To:	*Valerie Glines Daniell*
Sent:	*Friday, October 13, 2000 9:29 PM*
Subject:	*Wow, The Past*

Well, Hello,

What a lot of stuff has happened to you lately. Paralyzed for 6 months? You, the dancer? I have to hear more about that. I can only imagine a small morsel of what that might have been like.

Living in Georgia with my wife, three kids (girls), five dogs (Springers) and two cats (Mutts).

Work for a company in Phoenix as their North American Sales Director and travel all over the continent. This year it has averaged three weeks a month and the hope is that next year it will be a little less. Love it. Took me a while, and although it is somewhat physically demanding, being away that often (just during the week, home on weekends) makes my seven-day home-week very relaxing and peaceful. Work out of the house you know and don't exactly race around and I get to play the piano a lot.

I get out west two or three times a year and it would be great to take you out to dinner. I don't know when my next scheduled visit is, but I could give you 4-6 weeks notice and if you would like to get together just let me know.

You were one of the most important people that came into my life and I'm so glad that you wrote me. When I saw you at the reunion way back when, I was disappointed that I could not break away, if for no more than a few moments, and say a better hello.

At least write and tell me about your amazing experience.

John

But it turns out to be a false start. Valerie writes back and says she'd love to have dinner with John if he ever comes through Denver. But her reply doesn't come soon enough. Right at that time John switches jobs—and thus his email address—and so never gets her response. Disappointed, and assuming she has no interest in such a meeting, he clings to his pride and does not write again.

Over the next several years, Valerie calls Atlanta Information searching for a John Carpenter. She finds and dials plenty of them, but not the one she wants. After some weird exchanges, she calls it quits. The two seem fated to never connect.

The year 2003, however, changes all that.

Sixteen — Pas de Deux

Dancing shoes
Though the distances divide us
There's a paradise inside us
We can't lose

Me and you
Dance a 'pas de deux' forever and
I pray you never
Shed your dancing shoes

Dan Fogelberg - Dancing Shoes

Saturday morning, April 26, 2003, arrives bringing Valerie nothing worthwhile other than the norm: one of the two mornings each week when she can stay in bed, not have to struggle to get to work, drag herself back home, or cope with business bureaucracies.

She stays in bed until almost nine and rises slowly—as much due to her enjoyment of the luxury as to her injuries. After breakfast she gets in front of a computer and checks emails, while munching on a few of the M&Ms she keeps handy by the desk. An oldies radio station plays *Something* by The Beatles. A thought passes in which she recalls John Carpenter.

One email is from a Langley classmate, Bill Johnston. Valerie is one of many recipients—all classmates. Bill is sharing his discovery of a web site for the class. One can go there, create a log-in, and enter information about themselves, updating their classmates on their lives and contact info. MySpace and Facebook do not yet exist, so this website is a big deal.

Valerie signs up and scans the names. Under JOHN CARPENTER, she finds, along with a new email address for him: "Single again," and also the then-obsolete information that he's living in New Hampshire.

Her heart races. She immediately composes an email to him with the title, "I found you."

She writes:

April 26, 2003

John. I found you. I just signed up on the LHS alumni web site and saw your entry. The last time I heard from you, you were living in Georgia. How long have you been in New Hampshire? What are you up to now? All you wrote was "getting older, single again."

I am living in the Denver area and working at a local high school as a counselor. Since I last communicated with you in 2000 after breaking my neck, I have recovered more and am getting around much better. It has been an interesting journey. I now have a townhouse and I still have my forever faithful cat Bud. I don't know if you remember our exchange in 2000, but I was living in an apartment and working at the US Post Office Employee Assistance Program. I remember you said you traveled often and might be coming through Denver sometime. I responded that I would love to see you if you come through, but I never heard back from you. I am guessing from your alumni entry that you have been busy with many things in your life.

*I would love to hear from you if you should be so
inclined. I am really glad I found you. I tried to find
you recently by calling Information in the Atlanta area
but all the John Carpenter's were not you. Now I know
you were in NH. Interesting timing.*

I await your reply......

John writes her back the same hour. He brings her up
to date on the fracturing of his family. To which Valerie
immediately replies:

*"Wow, you have had a lot going on the past few years. It
seems we have much more to catch up on. Do you mind
if I call you now? If it's OK, what is your phone
number? I look forward to talking with you."*

They talk that same day for over three hours—which
isn't so long considering it's been 33 years since anything of
substance has passed between them. She's enthralled by his
voice.

By the end of the conversation they are caught up on
the facts of each other's lives. More significant is that serious
flirting has gone on between the lines.

The next morning, Sunday, the phone wakes Valerie.
John's voice.

"Good morning, did I wake you?"

"No, I was just laying here trying to get motivated to
get up."

"What are you doing Thursday?"

There's a pause before Valerie can completely shake
the cobwebs and dreams out of her head.

"*This* Thursday?"

"Yes."

"Um…Working?"

"I want to come see you Thursday."

Again. "*This* Thursday?"

Before John confirms that he does indeed mean this coming Thursday, Valerie resumes.

"You don't want to see me like this. It would be better if you just remembered me the way I was."

He chuckles. "No, really. I want to visit you. I can come for a long weekend. Hey, now is not the best time in my life either, but I really want to see you."

She surrenders—half excited, half-apprehensive—and agrees to pick him up at the airport on Thursday. She tells herself that, hey, at least they'll have a nice weekend. She can drive him into the mountains and show off the area's beauty while they reminisce. He'll realize that being with a disabled person is weird and they'll probably never see each other again, but, shoot, it will be good enough for a couple of days.

Thursday feels like summer, even though that season still lurks a month or two away. High school students flood out the doors, now free for the afternoon. The sun on the asphalt of the Littleton High School parking lot has raised the temperature to about 80 degrees as Valerie, four-prong cane at her side, clips across the pavement much faster than is her habit. She feels a drop of sweat wriggle past her lip and wonders if its cause is the heat or her excited agitation about what happens next.

She gets in the Bug and starts it up, aware of her own fluttering stomach and aware also that her mouth is dry. She reaches for a tin of breath mints and pops one just in case. She puts the car in gear, backs out of her space, shifts forward and heads for the airport.

She talks to herself throughout the drive. *You haven't felt like* this *for a long time. You've got this silly, childish "school girl" feeling. Like going on the first first-date… I wonder how he looks. What's he going to think when he sees me? What if this*

weekend turns out really awful? Get it together. Don't expect
anything. Just have a good visit. Think positive.

She pulls into an airport shuttle lane and there he is,
walking toward her, pulling a wheeled suitcase. He looks
different and yet the same. His hair is grey and nowhere near
as thick. He wears silver, round glasses, not his thick, black
frames of the Sixties. He's still tall and trim, just like in high
school.

Valerie gets out of the car and onto the walkway. John
leaves his suitcase where it is, goes to her and hugs her. It lasts
a good while and Valerie feels an old and comfortable
familiarity.

They don't need to exchange the usual pleasantries
about how good it is to see each other: that's understood.
John puts his suitcase in the back and gets in the car.

Here's the hard part. Right off the bat, Valerie must
share the reality, share just one of the hassles of her life. Too
bad, she thinks, that they just can't flow into something fun,
but it is what it is. So she just leaps into the long explanation:

"I have to go to physical therapy before we go home.
It won't take too long… I hope you won't mind hanging with
me while I do that. I go three times a week and can't miss it.
I go to this woman's house. Pam. She has Pilates equipment.
I've been working with her for about a year—but when I'm
finished, I have food at home. I'll cook you dinner, if you're
brave."

John smiles. "I can help. I love to cook."

He loves to cook.

As they drive, Valerie steals peeks at him. He still
looks handsome to her. She sees them in the Langley
auditorium, in his house, yelling at each other in the school
office… and kissing. She's so involved with memories that she
almost misses the turn to the physical therapist's house.

They pull up to the house. Valerie slowly emerges
from the car with the help of her cane. John comes around
and takes her arm as they walk towards the house. Pam, the

PT, greets them at the door and leads Valerie to the workout room.

Suddenly, Valerie feels that her movements, which up to now seemed pretty fluid all things considered, are surprisingly clunky and awkward. She feels like she's being watched by an entire auditorium of dance critics on opening night and realizes that, for the first time, John will see just how difficult it is for her to move around. A negative thought pokes through her defenses: *This was a big mistake. I'm going to look like a fool.*

Her warm-up exercises start on the mat table, but just now she simply sits on it like a kid waiting at a bus stop.

"I can help with your routine," John says brightly. "What can I do to help?"

Valerie, suddenly relieved, thinks: *You just did.*

John, she realizes, isn't one of those people who mistakenly think that disabled folks don't want help, or are bound by some misplaced pride in trying to do everything for themselves. He knows that, like anyone else who, say, might have a twisted ankle, she'd love some help now and then.

Valerie smiles. "I think you can just sit and watch."

"What is this contraption?" John points at a seat with springs.

"It's a resistance device."

"You going on that?"

Valerie nods.

"Let me help you get on it."

John helps her on, and then he sits on the floor and watches Valerie workout, with no more awkwardness than two old friends sharing a drink.

They joke about Valerie's "goofy" body and her need to get stronger.

Valerie goes through the whole workout, including a Pilates regimen. After an hour she's had enough. John sits next to her and puts his arm around her shoulders.

At Valerie's house, John drinks a Coors, while she drinks a red wine and arranges the makings for a stir fry dinner. Though Valerie is still self-conscious about her movements, John doesn't seem to notice. His face beams in a perpetual grin. They chop vegetables together like some couple that has been preparing meals together for decades.

Now a feeling of comfort surrounds her. Perhaps this will all work out.

After dinner, they clean up together, then move to the living room and sit side by side on the couch and make plans for the weekend.

The next day, Friday, is a work-day for Valerie. John drops her off at work and spends the day exploring local golf courses and sights. Meanwhile, Valerie arranges with the school's band/music teacher to let John sit down at one of the department's pianos—she desperately wants to hear him play again.

When John arrives to pick her up in the afternoon she says, "I have a surprise for you. The music teacher said you could play the school's piano—if you want. Do you? I'd love to hear you play."

"Absolutely. Let's go."

They walk to the high school's band room and Valerie almost feels like she's floating, she's that excited by the prospect of hearing him play again.

A few students hang around the band room but quickly exit when they see the two adults. John runs his hand along the instrument's side walls, then sits down and plays a few notes, testing the action of the keys. Then he starts to play. In a few minutes, the kids return, just to stand and listen.

Valerie's eyes mist over, but she's smiling nonetheless.

John pauses and looks at her as if to say, "Was that okay?"

Valerie keeps smiling and says, "Do you remember the song you composed for me when I was in Boston?"

"This one?"

He plays *The Serpent* without hesitation as though he'd been practicing it all these years. In an instant Valerie is a dancer again and a choreographer studying at the Conservatory. She feels as though she's carried his music in her soul from a time even before they'd met.

It dawns on Valerie that, for the first time in three— no, 30— years, she's having fun.

The next day provides more of it.

They decide to drive through the mountains to visit the Breckenridge Brewery on Saturday. Besides the views, John loves beer. After that, they'll visit an equestrian friend of Valerie's who lives in the eastern flatlands and perhaps have dinner with her.

Again, the weather is unseasonably perfect—a clear blue sky, sun and the smell of spring. They head west into the mountains—still covered in snow—and arrive in Breckenridge about an hour later. They sit at an outdoor table looking straight up at a 14,000-foot mountain peak; they could as well be in the Swiss Alps. They eat lunch and John samples the beers. He discovers one he loves called "Avalanche."

After lunch they drive down another mountain pass to a place where the turns straighten out and reveal a spectacular valley vista with visibility of 100 miles or more.

John leans forward. "My God. Let's pull over. I have to get out and soak this up."

Valerie pulls off the road. They get out of the car and stand enthralled by the open range. John puts his arm around her.

"I'm not sure I've ever seen you so happy," Valerie observes.

John looks down and smiles sheepishly. "Well, it's nice being here…with you. The state looks pretty good too."

"I'm glad you came."

"You know, what's weird is that when we were in high school I had a dream that I was playing the piano on top of a mountain in Colorado—and I had never been to Colorado."

The couple gets back in the car and resumes the trip. When they encounter a rare stop light, John takes Valerie's hand and says, "I want to be with you."

She's not sure how to take that and just stares. He goes on.

"I don't know how or when we can work it out, but I really want to be with you. We've lost so much time. We have to start making up for it. Right now."

Valerie pulls the car to the side of the road and tries to catch her breath and think. Finally she says, "Why would you want to take on life with a person like me? A person with a spinal cord injury?"

"We can deal with it," he insists. "You are still *you*. You're the sweetest person I've ever known, or will know. We could have a life of adventure together. Let's figure out a way to make it work."

"What if I don't get better? I might not, you know. You don't want to be looking after me all the time. You won't be able to do the kinds of things you love. You—"

"Hold on. I'm not proposing being with you predicated on the idea that you're going to get better. In fact, I go into this assuming you *won't* get any better and, moreover, that you'll probably get worse. Otherwise, under some conditional arrangement, if you didn't recover, I'd be gone— Now I'm not saying don't *try* to get better: always try. But I'm in this for better or worse. For me that's what real love is."

"Some people just can't handle being a caregiver all the time. It doesn't mean they don't love."

"I don't know about other people. I'll admit that without *real* love, nobody could handle it. But I've loved you since high school. And I *can* handle it."

And right there everything changes again. Just like that. But this time for the better. The weekend flies past them in a blur. Marathon talk sessions over beer and wine, during which Valerie actually pinches herself to make sure it's not all some dream. It seems that there just might be life after a catastrophe; it seems that her pep talks to herself just might have been true. Love returns.

After that first weekend, John nearly becomes a Boston-Denver commuter. In between, a flood of emails and phone calls fill in the gaps.

From one of John's emails, sending Valerie his itinerary:

From: John Carpenter
To: valerie daniell
Sent: Friday, May 07, 2003 6:20 PM
Subject: Oh, Hello

....And now down to business:
Friday, May 16, 2003
United flight #403 Departing 8:00AM Boston
Arriving 10:22AM Denver

Monday, May 19, 2003
United flight #348 Departing 10: 17AM Denver
Arriving 4:09PM Boston

Friday, May 23, 2003
Departing 4:30 PM Boston
Arriving 6:53 PM Denver

Tuesday, May 27, 2003
Departing 3:45 PM Denver
Arriving 9:33 PM Boston

Swoosh..................And I'm there again.

Next email:

I'm just sitting here, looking at you and me in front of that wall and smiling and thinking just how recently it was that I had such a bleak outlook on life. As to the "would you have stayed in your business forever?" How could that be true since things have changed and I am no longer staying in my "business"? That's the really cool thing about how I have lived my life. Since I can remember, I have allowed for the present to change my perception of the future. Rather than accept that there is no way to find happiness, I at least have been constantly open to the idea that it could come somehow. And here you are.

God I love you, I only hope I can give to you the happiness you deserve. Off to eat some dinner
Call me soon.

After those visits:

I just got out of the tub, reading more Morrie, putting it down and thinking of how we should go forward.

It seems to me that we have chosen to devote ourselves to each other, now, not in the past. And that we should stop talking about what happened, but what will happen. I'm more interested in what you think about the war in Iraq, the fact that in India there is still in place a caste system in place that horribly oppresses millions simply based on their birth, what colors you would want our new room downstairs to be, how can we both do better with our lives.

I want to explore, not repave, the road to the past.

Yes, who we were makes us who we are, but now we must go forward and let the past dissolve.

You are right, this is a giant move I am about to make. And I question every day if I am going about this the right and proper way. Keeping the fear at bay and not allowing it to cloud my true feelings is not a simple task. I have created so many "unknowns" for myself here and sometimes it gets the best of me and makes me worry. I know that this change will forever alter my relationship with my children, and Cleaves of course. What I have done in the past two years has already strained those relationships, and it isn't easy knowing that. Somewhere in my heart I know they will not stop loving me, but the fear of such a major shift in my life causes me to worry that they will hate me. I also believe that that emotions will surface regardless of how things pan out in the long run, it is only human nature, and I have to muster the strength to live through that time.

Also, here is my opportunity to decide what I really want to do with my life. Hard to do. I have lived for so many years setting aside my desires to provide for others. I've forgotten what it feels like to wake up in the morning, being passionate about my "work," whatever it might be. It for so long has simply been "get through the day."

No more questions about my resolve.

No more worrying that I might leave you as others had done.

Please understand that sometimes in the next few weeks I will simply be awash in thoughts that I can't quite express, simply because I don't know all the answers now. This list, although finite, seems endless. So much to sort out in such a short period of time.

And this hasn't been long in the planning. This is such a sudden shift that every day my head spins a bit, and I have to look very deeply into my heart to find the courage to make this happen.

I know our life will be beautiful.

I know the peace we will find with each other.

In what seemed impossible just a year before, Valerie moves to Massachusetts to live with John. Seven years later they would marry.

Massachusetts

Before leaving Colorado, Valerie finds a counseling job in Massachusetts at "The Walden School." The school is a program connected to The Learning Center for the Deaf in

Framingham. They happen to be looking for a Clinical Director to coordinate "...mental health services for emotionally and behaviorally challenged deaf students in a residential treatment program." The job includes, "Supervising five clinicians for a student population of 30, ages eight through 21." Perfect.

After that she gives notice to her Colorado employers, sells her home, packs up and, with John and her cat, climbs into her yellow VW and road-trips it across the country to Lowell, Massachusetts. They arrive at John's rented apartment on June 1, 2004.

The apartment, part of an old-brick, converted mill, serves as their foothold until they can find something to buy.

In mid-August they find a house in Framingham, a suburb of Boston, about 26 miles from the city. But it's not exactly a dream home. Valerie remembers it as "an overpriced dump."

The place is a ranch house relic from the Sixties when all the homes on the street were stamped from the same form. This one has peeling wallpaper, flooded carpets damp with mold and mildew, no doors on the bathrooms, an inch of grease on the kitchen floor, flaking exterior paint, original 1960s kitchen appliances, and a washing machine sitting in the kitchen.

But it has potential and a big yard. Besides it sits less than a mile from Valerie's new job and her rehab facility.

Sold.

The risk is not as bad as it seems. John Carpenter has the skills to renovate the place and earns his namesake. He guts the kitchen, redesigns and rebuilds it in a way that would make *The Property Brothers* show proud. He installs new carpet, paints inside and out, builds a laundry room and after that, when his daughter, Hilary, comes to live with them, builds a bedroom for her just off the new laundry area.

People marvel at the transformation and word of John's skills circulate. Which is a good thing because his Value

Added Marketing company crashes and closes. In its place, John begins to get remodeling jobs all over the area. He tosses his tools into a minivan and becomes an all-purpose handyman—The Honey Do Man—with a waiting list of jobs. He goes from one major job to another building kitchens, bathrooms, staircases, and siding.

Meanwhile, Valerie's job at Walden School suits her skills and experience. Many of the school's deaf children have no families. Some are adopted—and then *un*adopted. Not that they're all adorable or easy to live with. They present ongoing crises. They climb on the roof and threaten to jump, break windows, mutilate themselves, attempt suicide, or runaway.

Valerie's hands are improved enough that she can sign and be understood. She's not as fast or fluid as before, but she's good enough. She manages the therapists, coordinates psychiatrist visits, runs the weekly team meetings and meets with various outside agencies such as the state's Department of Education and Social Services. She admits or declines to admit new students. She hires and fires therapists—all of them new graduates from counseling programs around the country. Some come from Gallaudet, like Valerie. She's on call 24/7. She covers the shifts of therapists during the holidays. Right up her alley.

After work, Valerie goes to physical therapy at Spaulding Rehabilitation just down the street from the school.

Her principle therapist, Beth Grill, an attractive, middle-aged woman with dark blonde hair past her shoulders, has a doctorate in physical therapy and specializes in patients with spinal cord issues.

They work diligently, long and often, on core strengthening, sit-stands, extremity exercises, stretches, pain management, adaptive equipment use (canes, crutches, etc.), activities of daily living practice, energy conservation. The major goal being to regain full function, independent living and participation in all of life's activities. Goals not lacking in ambition.

Dr. Grill physically moves Valerie's limbs, massages her hands to keep the soft tissue soft. There's ultrasound, deep heat, and electrical stimulation.

Later, Dr. Grill will be asked what kind of a patient Valerie was, or if she ever had any concerns about Valerie not doing prescribed work, and how Valerie handled adversity.

She will reply: "Valerie was very motivated, will to do what was recommended to her… She actually participated in a gym outside of therapy that has special equipment… Valerie is one of the most highly motivated people that I've met… She handles adversity in a problem-solving type of way. She's inspirational."

Initially Valerie uses her four-prong cane to get around. One of the first things Dr. Grill says to her is, "It's time to get you off that thing." Shortly thereafter, Valerie uses a single point cane and is so proud, she buys an elegantly carved wooden one that any 19th century British aristocrat might have envied.

When her insurance lapses (an off-again/on-again thing), Valerie goes to another facility called Easy Motions and works with a physical trainer named John Vernon, a fit, middle-aged man with thinning hair.

His approach is to strengthen Valerie's entire body. Essentially a total body workout with an emphasis on the core because, he reasons, the core is where all motion originates. He relies on weight training and exercises that put Valerie in unstable positions to allow as many muscles as possible to become involved.

They work on a cable machine that puts her in a standing position, creating a more difficult workout. They use a Bosu Ball, which is essentially a half-ball, to create an unstable base. While on the ball she does extremity exercises.

She does cardio on a recumbent bike. He has her use the stairs to gain entry into the gym, never the elevator.

At the time, Walden School shoulders one particular oddity. Considering that it's a school for deaf and handicapped children, there is an astonishing lack of ADA-required accessibility features.

There are no handrails up the front staircase entrance. There are no bar-rails next to toilets in many of the buildings, no rails in the buildings at all. No ramps of any kind, anywhere. Rather than install such features, the federally-funded institution simply pays the fines.

Valerie's suggestions for handicapped-accessible accommodations are not implemented. When she repeats the suggestions she's branded a trouble-maker.

Otherwise life is good. They cruise the region on the weekends. They visit Cape Cod and Newport, checking out the mansions. John gets to hang with friend and Fog bandmate Jon Chase and jam in the recording studio John helped build.

They entertain a steady stream of visiting friends and family from all over the country. Valerie's brother comes from Alaska; John's parents come from Virginia, and Hilary.

At the end of each workday, John makes them gourmet, Continental meals of complex sauces and gravies— enough to almost make up for the miserable winter weather of the region. The weather seems to be always overcast, raining, cold, and humid which, by contrast to Colorado's lower humidity, can make a person homesick for the Rockies.

Nonetheless, John makes the home cozy with large fireplace blazes throughout the winter. They put a free-standing chiminea in the spacious back yard and, weather permitting, light some fires in that and enjoy their forest-encircled lot. From their backyard vantage they watch a parade of deer, wild turkeys, skunk, woodchucks, rabbits and feral cats.

In 2006, John's daughter Hilary comes to live with them—or more accurately, has been commanded to do so by John. It seems Hilary has become a wild-child, has made some terrible judgments, gotten into financial troubles, and must now be carefully shepherded.

But it's only one more thing. Nothing they can't handle.

Seventeen – Performance Enhancer

A promising opportunity arrives in 2005. Valerie's spinal cord specialist, Dr. Kevin O'Connor, tells her about a clinical drug trial about to be conducted for patients with spinal cord injuries—a drug developed by Switzerland's Sanofi-Aventis Pharmaceutical Company with the potential to amplify a patient's recovery process—help them walk.

"I have six patients who are participating now," he says. "One has been in a wheelchair for 12 years and now he's walking with a walker. The drug has been very helpful to *all* my patients."

Valerie immediately applies and is accepted—along with 270 other patients worldwide—as a participant in the second-stage, six-month trial of "HP 184," also known as Nerispirdine. As is customary, volunteers in a drug trial do not know if they actually are taking the drug or a placebo.

Dr. O'Connor takes baseline measurements, on a scale of one to five, of her muscle strength, walking ability, and pin-prick skin sensations. Most of her measurements are in the one-to-three range—not very high. She takes the pills every day for six months, and continues her regular workouts.

After the first month, Valerie takes another series of measurement tests, that reveal nothing significant. She says, "I'm noticing a greater appetite than before… And… my bladder is working right again. Is it possible I don't have the placebo?"

After the second month, Valerie is tested again. Dr. O'Connor places electrodes on her legs and feet to monitor the length of her steps and record how fast she walks. She walks for one minute, down the hall and back. Her numbers rise.

"What can you tell me about how you feel?" the doctor asks.

"I'm stronger. When I go to physical therapy I can do things I haven't been able to do since I broke my neck. I can walk up and down stairs one stair at a time instead of two feet on each stair. I can climb up and down the stationary ladder. It is amazing. I feel that I'm stronger everyday."

"Not surprised. Your numbers are going up. Let's see how you do next month."

Valerie enjoys dramatic improvement in the strength of her legs and thighs. Her bodily functions work properly. She finds herself on an emotional tightrope. She wants to scream out a cry of jubilation—but maybe that cry will wake the sleeping gods of disappointment and strike her down. Still… holy shit.

She walks up and down stairs easily and moves with some grace once again. She can walk a few steps without any cane at all. Her physical therapist, eyes bugging out and mouth agape—and not knowing about the test, jokes, "What have you been taking? You're killing it here."

No way she's taking the placebo—or if so, keep it coming.

At the end of the trial, Valerie gets a phone call from Dr. O'Connor's assistant.

"We have news on your study. You were taking 400 mg's of the drug, which is the highest dosage. So it was no placebo."

Valerie's can't contain a broad grin. "When does it go on the market?" she asks.

"This is the second trial on the fast track for FDA approval. It was manufactured for people with Multiple Sclerosis but they wanted to see if it helps spinal cord injured people—and evidently it does. We'll let you know when we have more information."

But the information doesn't come. The trials have ended, that's all anyone knows.

Ten days after she stops the drug, Valerie wakes, gets out of bed and finds herself considerably weaker and unstable. She tests herself by doing some "sit-stands" at the bed's edge. No. It's not there. Her newly-found strength has ebbed away like that of Samson shorn.

She writes to Sanofi-Aventis, then calls them in hope that they'll let her continue the drug while awaiting FDA approval. Request denied. But what about just on humanitarian grounds? She knows it works. Request denied. Well, what were the results of the trial? No comment.

She and other members of the trial jump to online chat rooms trying to find out if anyone knows anything about this ray of hope that has suddenly gone dark. The conversations go like this:

kathyingwersen

April 23, 2007 at 9:43 pm · 6 replies

Hi, I'm new to the site. I live in Australia. Last year I was one of 270 world-wide spinal cord injured people undergoing stage 2 of the drug HP 184. I am a C5/6 quad, 6 years post injury, motor complete. I hd a fantastic response to the drug with increasing significant motor and sensation improvements. Aventis decided to run stage 3 in America and was recruiting there late last year. Since then nothing. Does anyone know if this drug is progressing to stage 3 trials or has it been shelved. Aventis will not answer my emails on the subject and the researchers who ran the stage 2 trial here are also unable to find out anything from them. Apparently by law the drug company must reveal if there were any adverse side effects and this has not happened. So there is a drug out there which can help some people as a treatment, (all improvements disappear within 3 days of stopping the drug) and which seems to have been dropped by Aventis for some reason, I suspect commercial. Anyone know anything...?

Tiffiny

April 24, 2007 at 3:17 pm
So, aventis might have discovered some ill side-affects to the drug you took and they're not telling you? scary.

what kind of motor and sensation improvements did u see?

tiff

---

kathyingwersen

April 25, 2007 at 8:11 pm

No I don't think there were any contraindications re the drug, at least none were reported on the net from participants, rumour was that while some had significant improvements they were not in sufficient numbers to make the drug company continue with developing the drug. But we don't know. Aventis has dropped the drug from their web site. My improvements were improved bladder and bowel control, increased sensation, movement in feet, toes, and legs where none were before, these improvements increased over the 6 months of the trial and were monitored over that period

by the medical team here in Sydney. When the trial
finished, everything went over 3 days, it was devastating.

---

bjoy

June 30, 2007 at 7:30 pm

I just read your last entry. I have never heard of this
drug in America, I am a nurse and my daughter is a
quad, C5-6. I would say it probably was very expensive
and they couldn't make it last so they may still be
working on it. I'm so sorry you had to give up your
improvements, but I'm sure you will be contacted if they
want to do further testing. If you do hear from them
please let us know. Blessings Bjoy

---

kathyingwersen

June 30, 2007 at 9:21 pm

Hi Bjoy, I feel I am a lone voice crying in the wilderness,
there is a treatment out there for SCI and Aventis is
denying it to us. All 8 of us doing the Sydney trial had
the drug, no placebos, and all had improvements. I
think your faith in Aventis doing the right thing, as
opposed to the commercially correct thing is totally
misplaced. We were the guinea pigs, we took the risks, as
did participants in all the other countries that were part
of the stage 2 trial, we were promised that we would be
given preference in participating in the much larger
planned stage 3 trial. Instead of this Aventis pulled the
plug, firstly by stating stage 3 would be held exclusively

in USA excluding all of the countries where the Stage 2
trials had been held, then by pulling the plug on the
continued development of the drug altogether. If you
want to know more follow-up with CareCure forum
thread relating to this subject. Aventis doesn't even have
the good manners to reply to my emails. I travelled
almost 500 kilometers each time of 8 times in order to
participate in this trial and underwent a massive loss of
all gained function when it ended, I feel very let down
by Aventis' indifference to me and more important to all
of us who could have been helped by this drug treatment.
My good wishes to you and to your daughter...regards
Kathy.

---

sheraphics

May 6, 2009 at 8:37 am
Here are a couple of websites I have found about a
woman who was in the study in Boston and another
about the study, but no study results. Maybe you could
contact her and you could work together finding out
what happened. She wanted to continue also with good
results.

The woman referenced in the last thread, of course, is Valerie.

None of those in the trials has any idea why such an effective drug simply vanished. The results of Sanofi-Aventis's second trial remain unavailable. Web pages that showed the positive outcomes of their first trials have inexplicably disappeared. To date, the company says nothing more than that the trials are discontinued.

Valerie, like all the others, is left hanging; brought to the brink, within sight of The Promised Land, then yanked back.

Eighteen — Dark Reprise

On Sunday, January 21, 2007, two women arrive at Dallas-Fort Worth International Airport separately, both bound for Boston aboard American Airlines flight 654. One woman is returning from a family visit; the other, is heading off on a business trip.

The latter, a short, thin woman with Asian features, Rita Mohsin, Director of Information Services for the Federation of State Medical Boards, has a presentation to make on behalf of the Federation the following day in Concord, New Hampshire. Her presentation is entitled "Common License Application Form"—something used in the company's "Trusted Agent Platform."

She checks her luggage, but keeps a large, wheeled bag with her and rolls it through the airport until stopped at security. The line barely moves. She checks her watch. She's running a little late, but there's still plenty of time to make the flight. Per company policy, Mohsin used its travel agency to book the flight and, per company requirement, is traveling on Sunday in order to arrive in time for the presentation and spend only the minimum on lodging. If left to her own devices, she might have booked another flight—or day for that matter. Saturday would have given her a full day of rest before the meeting—but hey, the company's paying for the trip, so Sunday travel it is. Anyway, the trip is strictly business.

The other woman is Valerie. She's returning to Boston after visiting her parents. Airline personnel meet her at curbside with a wheelchair and check her baggage for her. Though Valerie now walks quite well with a single cane, she uses a wheelchair to get through the long, tiring—not to mention dangerous—bustle of airport crowds. An airline representative wheels her through the airport to the gate and, because of her condition, she is seated before the other passengers. She gets a seat behind the bulkhead of the plane, next to the aisle.

Valerie makes herself comfortable, takes an in-flight magazine from the seat pocket and browses stories while the rest of the passengers file in.

Mohsin shuffles in later with the rest of the crowd, dragging her suitcase behind her. She nears her seat—just behind Valerie's— bends down, lifts her bag—which weighs perhaps 20 to 25 pounds—and hoists it upward with two hands, placing it about half way into the overhead compartment just above Valerie. The case teeters, but rather than push it in further or rebalance it, Mohsin begins to take her seat.

Before Mohsin even sits, the bag falls out of the bin and slams Valerie in the head. A woman in a nearby row exclaims, "Oh my God."

A bright light sears Valerie's eyes, accompanied by a stabbing, electrical jolt that sizzles through her neck and body. She cries out in pain. She can't move. Something has happened but, like the victim of an assassin's bullet, she has no idea what's hit her. But something terrible has happened. The horror materializes in her mind—almost too terrifying to attach words to it: she's paralyzed again.

A weird thought races through her head: *please God don't let me go back to Baylor.* A flood of other thoughts and emotions jostle for her attention: *This can't be happening… got to get home… got to see John… Don't let me be paralyzed, not again. Suddenly. Just like that. Back to Square One. After all that work. This is a dream. Must be.*

The pain persists. She tries to move her hands, fingers and feet. Nothing. Then, after some minutes, the fingers budge—a little.

Mohsin, meanwhile, remains in her seat, reading a magazine. She does not get up to see if Valerie is hurt, much less offer assistance, in fact, she does not even rise to retrieve her suitcase. She actually chuckles.

At the same time, Greg Sconce, a business traveler sitting across the aisle and one row behind Valerie, immediately calls for the flight attendants, who arrive in seconds.

"Are you okay?" one asks.

Valerie bleeds from her brow. She shakes. Tears roll down her face.

"No. No, I"m not. I'm hurt."

The attendants divide their duties. One patches Valerie's wound. Another asks other passengers if they'd seen what happened, and takes their names. Another brings ice. Another writes down Valerie's symptoms and her account of what happened. Another asks Mohsin for her name and her side of the story. Mohsin refuses to give either, or to answer any questions. Later, Mohsin will try to hide her involvement by telling American Airlines not to release the accident report to Valerie.

While this unfolds, Valerie squirms in her seat to see if she can move anything else. The plane's doors close and it pushes back from the gate.

Valerie needs to shout if she's going to get off the plane now. But this is Dallas, and no, she isn't staying here, not so close to Baylor. Oddly, given the circumstances, she recalls some factoid that airlines must spend thousands of dollars for each minute of delay, and Valerie—go figure—doesn't want to be the cause of that. She's going to Boston or die in the air.

Once airborne, an attendant goes forward and tells the captain about the accident. He radios Boston and makes sure Valerie is met by a supervisor and a wheelchair.

John meets her at the airport as she's wheeled into baggage claim. The second Valerie sees him she starts to cry.

***

Valerie doesn't want to go to the hospital, so they drive home, ice her neck and lie down. The pain gets worse.

The following morning, they call her primary care doctor who sends her in for an immediate MRI.

The imaging shows nothing broken, but a knot the size of a golf ball on her neck. The doctor tells her to see her spinal cord specialist, Dr. O'Connor—ASAP.

After examining Valerie, Dr. O'Connor says she has suffered additional damage to her spinal cord. Regular ultrasounds are ordered.

The neck pain continues unabated as the weeks go by. Though Valerie can stand and move, she notices a marked decline in her capacity to do so. Her hands begin to lose their facility. Her feet and her fingers go numb, on and off. Her left hand goes into "curling" like a claw. Her right hand spasms. She has increasing difficulty using sign language. Her back goes into spasm. Her physical therapist notes a decreased range of motion in her neck, decreased motor strength. Valerie starts dropping items soon after picking them up. Her left foot starts to drag, toe down, when taking steps.

She continues physical therapy, determined as ever, but each session, and each time she walks, her neck pain rises to such a level that she nearly passes out. The ongoing level of pain is such that she cannot sleep. All the progress she made over the past seven years is deteriorating.

Through it all, Valerie tries to continue working.

***

An important meeting is scheduled at Walden School for the week after Valerie's return from Dallas. It's being held in the basement of one of the school's buildings, formerly an old barn, now used as a conference room.

To get in the basement, one parks at the top of a hill and walks down an incline that has no railings. The incline is carpeted in wet leaves and dirt from winter rain. The entrance to the barn itself is via its original heavy, rusty sliding door. Even when relatively fit, Valerie could never move the door on her own; someone else always had to help her slide it. Normally, she would hobble in with her cane and try not to slip on the mud or dirt, then try to ease herself into one of the room's rickety, armless, plastic chairs.

The day before the meeting, Valerie asks the school's assistant director if they had installed any support rails in the old barn bathroom. No. Despite requests and ADA fines over other issues, the school just hadn't gotten around to it.

Valerie asks if she can be excused from the meeting and send someone in her place. The director says yes.

A few days later, Valerie arrives at work and goes into her boss's office for their usual weekly meeting.

She greets the boss and sits down across the desk from her. Instead of saying hello, the boss says, "Valerie, I think this is not working. I think this is not a good fit... I'm sorry."

The words hang in the air between them like a circling drone.

"I beg your pardon?

"It's just not a good fit."

"You're firing me?."

"Yes."

"Why? My work, my reviews, have been great."

"It's just not a good fit."

"But why?"

"It's just not a good fit."

A full minute passes.

Valerie feels her eyes watering, but fights down her emotions. She takes a breath.

"I'll wrap things up, then. I assume you're giving me two weeks."

"No, I want you to leave right now. Give me your pager and keys. You can come back on the weekend and clean out your office."

Valerie has never been fired in her life. It's clear to her what has happened: they want to replace her with someone who has fewer needs.

When she tells John later, he's stunned by the volume and fury in her voice. She never yells and yet here she is, roaring.

"Dammit, they had a guy on staff who'd been charged with *child abuse*. They gave him two—*two*—weeks' notice and a damned going away party."

"What do you want to do?"

"I want to get the hell out of here. Boston sucks. I want to go back to Colorado."

John just smiles. "I was hoping you'd say that."

Valerie starts to cry.

May 2007 finds Valerie, John and Hilary in Denver where Valerie—no surprise—starts over from Square One. Surgeries, rehab, physical therapy: she's going to come back she tells herself. It won't be easy, or course. It never is. But it's even tougher now. Money is tight. Insurance comes and goes.

And one more tragedy awaits.

Nineteen — Dying Swan

... The wild swan's death-hymn...
... was low, and full and clear...
Sometimes afar, and sometimes anear;
But anon her awful jubilant voice,
With a music strange and manifold,
Flow'd forth on a carol free and bold...

From The Dying Swan
Alfred, Lord Tennyson

John's daughter Hilary is 25 years old, but seems much younger. She has both the innocence and irresponsibility of a child—something that can be both endearing and maddening at the same time. She's the source of John's discovery some time ago that he is a deeply loving and caring man; someone who has the strength to care for others even though there's a toll to pay.

Hilary has an impish look to her. Her body is slight, her hair short, such that one might think of Scout in the movie version of *To Kill a Mockingbird.* Her eyes are narrow; the left one marked by a slightly lazy drift toward the center of her face—which adds to her pixyish charm. When on her own, she got in trouble—wrote some bad checks; probably unaware of the seriousness of the act—which is why she lives with John and Valerie, under John's close and caring gaze.

The family finds relief from its struggles with drives through the mountains. Sometimes all of them go, sometimes just John and Hilary. They take pictures of themselves at scenic pullouts with the state's snow-laden, spears of mountains punctuating the spaces behind them. Hilary always smiles—camera or no. She loves John and Valerie; and she loves being loved by them. She works at Target. Life is good.

***

Periodically, those with hydrocephalus who have shunts draining their accumulated fluid, must have parts of the system replaced or adjusted. It's thought of as a minor surgery—if such a thing exists. For Hilary, an increase in migraines means she needs a new valve to be inserted just above her ear.

It's a Friday in May. Sun warms the thin air; the sky is blue as a mountain lake. John drives Hilary to the hospital where they'll put in the valve and keep her overnight for observation.

"How you doing," he asks as they cruise through early morning traffic.

"I guess I'm as ready as I can be. I left my jewelry on the dresser... Actually, I'm pretty nervous. But I'm sure I'll be okay... Right?"

"Lean over here and give me a hug."

"You're driving."

"I don't care."

She laughs and carefully hugs her dad without pulling him off line.

John grins. "Listen, you'll be fine. I'll be there when you wake up."

When they get to the hospital, John accompanies his girl into the admitting area and helps with the paperwork. The place looks like a Ritz-Carlton—beautifully decorated, new, comfortable furniture, tasteful artwork. The place is doctor-owned and opened just eight months earlier.

When it's time, a team escorts Hilary through double wide doors into the prep area. John waves at her and continues to do so even after the doors have closed and she is out of sight.

By the afternoon, John has gone home, picked up Valerie and returned to the hospital. There, the two of them wait for news of the procedure.

John rises when he sees Hilary's doctor come down the hallway toward them. The doctor motions for John to sit back down and then joins him in an adjoining seat.

"Everything went very well," he says, smiling. "The digital valve I put in should help regulate drainage nicely. I think it's going to reduce the number and severity of her migraines too."

John lets out a deep breath and only then realizes he hadn't exhaled since the doctor appeared.

"Great," he says.

"I am glad she agreed to do this," the doctor goes on. "I was concerned about her CAT scans. We'll need to have those more frequently. ... Anyway, she'll be in her room soon and you can see her there. Any questions, just have the nurse contact me."

A half-hour later a nurse arrives and waves to John and Valerie. They follow her slowly to the patient's room.

Hilary sits up in bed with a bandage wrapped around her head. She's groggy from the anesthesia but has a big smile on her face.

"Hi Dad, Hi Val. ... I feel weird."

Valerie smiles. "Believe me, I know. It will take you awhile to wake up. Do you want some ice chips?"

"I want some ice *cream*."

"Let's see what we can do."

John hails a nurse and relays the ice cream request.

"Can I call Jen and let her know I'm ok?"

John pulls the phone over to Hilary who dials the number.

John and Valerie wait patiently while Hilary and Jen —her best friend—chat and giggle. In the middle of the call, the ice cream arrives and Hilary gobbles it down and talks at the same time. Finally, Hilary says goodbye and hands the phone and the bowl back to John.

"We noticed that a lot of the rooms are empty," Valerie says. "I think you're the only patient on the hall. That means you'll be treated like a queen."

"Cool." Hilary smiles, but not as widely as before. Her eyes start to close with fatigue.

John strokes her bandage lightly. "Well, we'll let you rest. We'll be back to pick you up in the morning. Call us if you want anything."

Hilary nods and closes her eyes.

At 8:00 a.m. the following morning, the Carpenters' phone rings, John answers and hears:

"Mr. Carpenter, this is Colorado Orthopaedic. There's been an emergency. Please come right away."

Without waiting to hear more, John grabs his keys and rushes toward the door. He hollers over his shoulder.

"Something's up. Going to the hospital. I'll call when I know."

And he's gone.

Valerie wants to run after him, but can't. She puts aside her rising concern for Hilary and works out the logistics. She can call her girlfriend, Ali. It's Saturday, so she'll be home.

"Ali, I need your help. Something's happened at the hospital. John left in a rush. Can you come get me?"

Ali is there in 20 minutes. The two women are on the road two minutes later.

Enroute, Valerie's cell phone rings with a call from John.

"I don't know what happened yet, but Hilary is in a different hospital now—St. Joseph's— in their ER. It's the one across the street from where she was. No one's telling me anything except that she needed to be rushed over there. So meet me at St. Joseph's ER. Okay?... Something doesn't feel right, Val. It doesn't feel good."

In another 20 minutes, John, Valerie and Ali find themselves seated in the ER waiting room looking at a nurse.

"I am Amanda. Hilary will be moved to ICU in a few minutes... How much do you know?" she asks.

"We don't know anything. What's wrong? What's happened?" John tries to keep the panic out of his voice.

A doctor comes into the room and stands beside them. He asks the same question: "Mr. Carpenter, what do you know?"

"*I* don't know *anything?*. Why isn't anyone saying anything? What's happened?" John repeats, this time more edgy.

"We're not sure. We'll do some tests when she is settled in the ICU... Right now she is in a coma."

Valerie and John at the same time: "A *coma?*.."

The doctor and nurse hurry away before more questions can be launched at them.

Valerie, John and Ali move to the ICU's waiting room. A social worker joins them and introduces herself, then asks, "What do you know?"

John starts to lose it. "We... don't... know ANYTHING. *You* people should be the ones that know things, but no one's telling us anything. What is going on?."

"I am not sure, but the doctors will talk with you when Hilary is settled in her room."

"Bullshit. Something's wrong here."

John is about to unleash his frustrations on the social worker, when a door opens and a nurse motions toward them to come.

John, Val and Ali go into the ICU. Hilary lays on a bed and is connected to tubes, a ventilator and monitors. She is white as the sheets around her.

John holds Hilary's hand and kisses her forehead. He doesn't look up when he speaks.

"What is wrong with her?" he sobs.

The nurse shakes his head.

A doctor enters. He looks in Hilary's eyes.

"Seems like it might be drug related. We'll watch her closely. We'll call you as soon as we have information."

Valerie takes Hilary's hand; it is cold.

The Carpenters and Ali leave and walk across the street to the original hospital to pick up Hilary's personal items.

In the following hours, John calls his ex-wife Cleaves, and his other two daughters, Kristen and Page. Cleaves arranges to fly out immediately. But still no answers, or even prognoses, are forthcoming.

No one can eat or sleep.

Saturday turns into Sunday. Finally the doctor calls John with a grim update.

"Mr. Carpenter, we don't know exactly how it happened but Hilary is not going to make it. You need to consider taking her off life support. I'm so sorry."

John hears himself speaking, but it's as though he's listening to a recording of his own voice.

"I can't believe this is happening. What went wrong? When I left her after her surgery she was laughing and eating ice cream. Jesus Christ.... Her sisters are coming here from Georgia...." Then more quietly, "Is it possible you can keep her on the machines until they get here?"

"Well... it's not recommended, but I guess we can. When are her sisters coming?"

"Tuesday morning is the earliest."

"Well…" the doctor's voice sounds even more uneasy than before.

"What?"

"You know, Hilary was an organ donor, so we need to take care of that in a timely manner." Again, "I'm so sorry this happened… Would you like to talk with our social worker?"

"No."

Hilary is kept on life support until her sisters can arrive to say goodbye.

Weeks later the phone rings. A reporter is on the line.

"Is this John Carpenter, Hilary Carpenter's father? I'm Rick Sallinger with Channel 7 News."

"Yes, I'm John."

"I have some information to share. I'd also like to interview you in person. Is that possible?"

"What information?."

"Mr. Carpenter, have you read the Colorado Department of Health's report on the Colorado Orthopedic and Surgical Hospital?

***

The 114-page Colorado Department of Health report reads, in part:

June 2009.
Department of Health and Human Services

The hospital failed to meet 5 federal Conditions of Participation under 42 CFR 482. …among them

482.12(e)(1) CONTRACTED SERVICES
The governing body must ensure that the services performed under a contract are provided in a safe and effective manner.

... the governing body (the Hospital) **failed to ensure** the contractual agreements **for emergency response from an adjacent hospital were provided in a safe and effective manner** or within standards of practice.

Failure to ensure that this contractual agreement could be provided in a safe and effective manner **resulted in delayed response to a life-threatening decline in a patient's condition from which the patient did not survive**.

82.13 Patient rights - The hospital failed to ensure patients received care in a safe setting.

482.21 Quality Assurance Performance Improvement - The facility failed to have an on going process to evaluate and monitor the effectiveness of processes of care for the emergency services provided by contract and to evaluate the quality of the in-house emergency services.

482.23 Nursing Services - **The hospital failed to ensure nursing services were furnished by qualified, competent registered nurses in sufficient numbers** to meet the needs of all patients served.

482.55 Emergency Services - **The hospital failed to meet the emergency needs of its patients in accordance with acceptable standards of practice.**

These multi-system failures.... **in combination led to the inadequate monitoring, medication error, and lack of evaluation for side effects or effectiveness of medications administered, and contributed to the collapse and ineffective rescue by hospital staff for patient #20.**

Patient #20. Also known as Hilary Carpenter.

The Denver Post follows up with a series of articles. Among them:

Denver Post — July 17, 2009

172

REVIEW FOLLOWS PATIENT DEATH AT DENVER
HOSPITAL

By Karen Auge

Just before midnight May 14, Hilary Carpenter logged
on to her My-Space page.

"Surgery in the morning. Nervous to say the least," she
wrote. "Thoughts and prayers are more than
welcomed."

The next morning, the 25-year-old Arapahoe
Community College arts student checked into the
Colorado Orthopaedic and Surgical Hospital in Denver
to have a shunt valve in her brain replaced.

Five days later, she was dead.

As a result of her death, the state health department
took the highly unusual step of ordering the hospital,
which opened in September, to stop accepting patients
except in emergencies...

Drug "incorrectly" given

According to a report by state health investigators,
Carpenter complained of severe headaches and was
vomiting the morning after her surgery.

One of two registered nurses for seven in-patients who
were hospitalized that morning called a physician on
duty, who prescribed a drug for nausea and pain.

Carpenter was given Demerol, but according to state
investigators, "the medication was administered
incorrectly, with the wrong dose and wrong route."

When the nurse checked on her 15 minutes later,
Carpenter's heart had stopped.

What happened next, as state health department
investigators described it, was utter confusion.

"A crash cart was . . . brought to the patient's room, but staff were unfamiliar with the layout of its contents, and there was some initial confusion about where things were located," according to the state report.

The doctor on duty became frustrated with the situation and yelled at staff, exacerbating a situation the state inspectors described as "chaotic."

Poor emergency training

COSH has an agreement with the adjacent Exempla St. Joseph for the larger hospital to respond when needed in emergencies. However, the state found that when COSH personnel called them, St. Joseph staffers had trouble navigating the hospital and finding Carpenter's room.

Eventually, about 20 minutes after Carpenter was found not breathing, hospital staff called 911 and summoned paramedics to the hospital.

She was taken to St. Joseph and remained there until she was removed from life support May 19...

Later, another state report faulted the adjacent hospital, St. Joseph, for failures to ensure patient safety. Again, according to *The Denver Post*:

Report: St. Joseph endangered welfare of orthopedic patients
A state report says the hospital has erred sending patients to an adjacent orthopedic center.

By Jennifer Brown
The Denver Post

September 25, 2009

Review follows patient death at Denver hospital
Denver hospital hobbled after death probe

St. Joseph Hospital failed to ensure the safety of patients it sent to a doctor-owned orthopedic hospital where a young woman died because of a medcation error, according to a state report released Thursday.

The Denver hospital, criticized in the 76-page report for not providing enough oversight of the smaller Colorado Orthopaedic and Surgical Hospital, was forced to submit a correction plan to the state health department....

St. Joseph contracted with the neighboring orthopedic hospital for surgeries on about 380 patients, many of whom received joint replacements. In July, less than a year after it opened, COSH was asked by the state to stop performing surgeries...

St. Joseph was cited by the state Department of Public Health and Environment for neglecting to make sure the orthopedic hospital "met acceptable standards of care," including the ability to manage medical emergencies.

The state report details two incidents of chaotic and inappropriate care at the orthopedic hospital, including the May 18 death of Hilary Carpenter, a 25-year-old Arapahoe Community College arts student....

The orthopedic hospital has closed permanently... Exempla lost $3.9 million with the closure....

***

As a result of the tragedy, Colorado Orthopaedic & Surgical Hospital closes permanently. But Hilary is gone permanently. And the pain exists permanently.

Twenty — The Crucible

*"... Providence moves... a whole stream of events...
raising in one's favor all manner of unforeseen incidents,
meetings and material assistance, which no man could
have dreamt would have come his way."*

— *W. H. Murray, Scottish explorer.*

In the four years following the dropped suitcase
incident, Valerie's abilities steadily deteriorate. She cannot use
sign language—which means she cannot counsel the deaf,
cannot work. Her ability to walk—even with crutches—drops
to a point where a wheelchair is often the best way for her to
get around. Bodily functions return to their unpredictable
ways. Her sense of touch deadens. Spasticity returns at night.
Muscle strength deserts her. Exercise becomes impossible.
Medical bills, along with the costs of ordinary life, become
overwhelming. Coupled with the loss of Hilary, life reaches its
lowest point.

At the nadir of one's life, a choice presents itself: like
the theme in Valerie's first choreographed dance long ago:
Advance or Retreat? Suffer the slings and arrows of
outrageous fortune? Or take arms against them?

Valerie and John choose the latter.

Which is why February 15, 2011 finds Valerie and
John seated along the back spectator rows of the Earl Cabell
Federal Building Courthouse, of United States District Court,

Northern District of Texas, on the second day of the trial in the lawsuit they've brought against Rita Mohsin and, more important, her employers, the Federation of State Medical Boards; a suit that charges Mohsin and her company with the negligence that caused Valerie's colossal setback.

John sits at the edge of a row of bench pews. Valerie, in a wheelchair, is parked next to him. A few spectators are scattered around the other pews—habitual, amateur trial watchers, mostly retired folks who, instead of daytime tv, come to the courthouse for their entertainment. The day before, on the trial's first day, Valerie wore a red blouse—not because her lawyer advised it, but because, sentimentalist that she is, she observes Valentine's Day. Today, she's wearing a simple blue dress. Occasionally, she catches one of the spectators checking her out.

Valerie's attorney, Roy Payne, rises from the Plaintiff's Table—now piled with enough cardboard file boxes to build a fortress—and approaches the jury. Roy, a handsome, disarming man with thick, greying hair, bears a passing resemblance to the actor, Patrick Duffy. He speaks to the jury in a polite, earnest Southern accent—an attribute of his combined years in Virginia and Louisiana.

"Ladies and gentlemen, I have known Valerie for the better part of both of our lives. She is a caring and compassionate person who once used her love of dance to help deaf children. She became an interpreter for the deaf and then a psychotherapist, until a terrible accident in the year 2000 broke her neck and paralyzed her for a time— robbing her of her ability to help others... For seven years, I watched her fight to recover. And recover she did. Until January of 2007 when the negligent actions of the defendants in this case took that all away from her yet again."

Valerie watches Roy outline his case for the jury. She squirms in her chair, trying to find a comfortable position which is just not going to happen because, no matter what physical position might suit her, emotional stress will still wring her insides. Conflict and confrontation do not agree with her. On the other hand, the opponents have been so arrogant and lacking in common decency throughout this process that she does indulge a longing for justice… a longing for a little comeuppance—and she has a friend who can do it.

Roy delivers a shorter version of the case he outlined to the opposition two months earlier in his 117-page settlement offer—an offer which consisted of witness depositions, case law, anatomical diagrams, detailed descriptions of surgeries and their attendant pains, professionally estimated current and future medical bills, lost income calculations, loss of lifestyle and enjoyment calculations—everything documented by outside experts, down to the last penny. The total summary of damages came to $16,461,983 and 72 cents. Roy had offered to settle for $6,000,000 and warned the opposition that if they rejected the offer, he would ask for much more at trial. At the time, the other side countered at $250,000.

So now, Roy promises the jury that he will prove:

A. The facts of the incident: that Rita Mohsin's negligent actions caused a heavy suitcase to fall on Valerie's head;

B. That the incident caused Valerie's current physical deterioration;

C. That the law holds that Mohsin's employer is also responsible; and that they will;

D. Document the full extent of her losses both in dollars and cents and in pain and suffering.

"Ladies and gentlemen, Valerie is one of the best people you will ever hope to meet. Her life's goal is to help others. At the end of this trial, you'll be proud to have helped her."

Valerie reaches over and takes John's hand.

"Roy. He's—" She chokes up.

John says, "I know."

***

At first, the confidence and passion in Roy's statement buoys Valerie's spirits. But when the defense attorney speaks, she loses some of that borrowed strength. She can't help but wonder if this is going to be just another huge, heartbreaking waste of time—like the HP-184 trials, when so much hope poured through her, only to drain away. She scans the eight jurors, selected during yesterday's session. The jury consists of five men and three women: all white, middle- to upper-class conservatives—not the type known for being sympathetic to personal injury cases. During yesterday's examinations, one of the potential jurors declared, "Yes, I *do* have a view about personal injury lawyers—they're a bunch of ambulance chasers." The speaker became the third person to voice that bias, causing the judge, in an unusual move, to intervene and admonish the man and the group as a whole.

"Right now you know nothing about this case," said The Honorable Judge Jeff Kaplan. "You have no basis to be drawing such conclusions. None of you do. As for you sir, you are discharged by me for cause."

Judge Kaplan, a small, wiry man in his late fifties with dark, curly hair and eyes that seem intensely focused on everything he regards, discharged four potential jurors himself.

During a pause, Roy whispered to his partner Sam Gregorio, who conducted the examinations for their side, "I wish Kaplan hadn't done that. Now they'll clam up and we won't know who's what." At the end of the day, Sam discharged three candidates: his limit. Even so, the man who becomes the jury foreman is the Chief Financial Officer of a large pharmaceutical company—an industry beleaguered by personal injury suits. The defense discharged no one.

Valerie took it personally—not so much because it bode ill for her case (which it did), but because the candidates' comments made her feel that fingers pointed at her, that the citizenry accused her of being some kind of fraud. She wanted to get up and cry to everyone, then and there, "I'm not like that. I'm a decent person."

Now sitting in for the trial's second day, she thinks, "We're going to lose. They already hate us." She looks away from the jurors and glances at the defense table. A thin blonde, 40-something woman in a tight grey business suit sits with the attorneys, but does not appear to be one of them. She turns toward Valerie and glares.

Valerie looks away and focuses on Roy and Sam. She recalls that Roy told her to prepare for personal attacks. He could see it coming. He knows what he's doing. She ignores the blonde woman and calms herself with the faith that her attorneys are very, very good—and deeply, personally, committed to her. She holds back her indignation and fear and instead, thinks back to the first discussions she had with Roy and Sam; back what seems like ages ago now.

***

Valerie Glines Carpenter (still referred to as Valerie Daniell during the trial) has been, throughout her life, a good person; always kind and caring for others. She has always kept in touch with those she loves. She finds that those qualities have given rise to what the Scottish explorer once described as "a whole stream of events... raising in one's favor all manner of unforeseen incidents, meetings and material assistance." Friends she has made over the decades have rallied to her side, brought together by a lifelong series of serendipitous coincidences.

To wit:

1. Right after the Sedona catastrophe, Lori Fuller, Valerie's playmate from childhood, learns from her sister Mariel, who is coincidentally Valerie's initial nurse in Flagstaff, that Valerie has broken her neck. Lori contacts Valerie and, over the months that follow, encourages Valerie

through uplifting calls. She brings her family to Baylor to visit Valerie in the rehab unit.

2. John Carpenter, while at Langley High School, has few friends, but one of them is a kid named Roy Payne, a studious, well-mannered, introverted type who shares with John a strange and dangerous interest in malicious mischief. Such activities create lifelong bonds—that is, if they don't land you in jail or in juvie. Fortunately, the two boys reform themselves in time and their friendship endures over the decades.

3. Roy and Lori did not meet while at Langley High School and certainly didn't date then. But they did meet later, coincidentally, during their college years. They married and had children. Theirs being the family that visited Valerie at Baylor.

4. News of Valerie's second injury from the dropped suitcase and her subsequent deterioration reaches Lori and, thus, reaches Roy.

5. Roy, of course, occupies a strong position to do something about the problem. In the intervening years since high school, Roy became a U.S. Federal Judge (close your eyes and say it aloud: "Judge Roy Payne") and now, after stepping down from the bench, he is engaged in private practice—in a Louisiana firm specializing in… personal injury.

With John tied up in construction contracts, Valerie travels, with her sister and brother-in-law, to Shreveport to see Roy.

The offices of Gregorio, Gregory and Payne sit among what appear to be single-story brick residences that suggest a type of Colonial motif: not just their brickwork, but their exterior faux shutters that hang outside vertical, rectangular windows that look like gun ports on an old ship.

Valerie, on crutches, enters and finds that the offices are not at all spacious—not what she expected—there's a tiny lobby with some chairs, a reception desk, and a glimpse down a narrow hallway with doors—presumably offices—on either side.

"You must be Valerie," the receptionist says cheerily, before Valerie can utter a word; she's meaning to be friendly, but inadvertently has underlined the fact that Valerie and her crutches stand out.

Valerie is about to say hello, when she hears her name. "Val."

It's Lori, the sight of whom takes Valerie momentarily back in time to the simple escapes they enjoyed as girls playing in the fields behind their Virginia homes. Whatever apprehension Valerie might have felt going into a law office, now vanishes. She's among friends. Great friends. They hug for a long while.

Roy is next. He too greets Valerie with a gentle hug and says, "Welcome to the Deep South. Let us show you around. It's not much, but we'll be moving soon."

They go slowly down the corridor as Roy points out the locations of the bathroom, kitchenette, copying machine and finally the conference room.

He sweeps his hand toward that room and says, "Why don't we all go in here and get comfortable? My partner Sam will join us momentarily. I have some Mediterranean salads coming. I hope those'll be okay?"

Valerie nods her assent.

The conference room is small and dark, furnished only with a single table and chairs. No credenzas, no video-conferencing screens, no telephones—just the table and chairs. Spartan. Focused.

The three friends sit and catch up on routine topics while they await the salads and Sam. In a minute, Sam arrives. He smiles, walks over to Valerie and takes her hand.

Until he speaks, Sam—a brilliant lawyer with 37 years experience in personal injury suits—looks as though he could be some too-diligent accountant who labors thanklessly in some gloomy New York City cubicle. And, in fact, he has a particular expertise in dealing with accountants and financial experts in the course of assessing damages. His hair, what's left of it, is grey and limited to the sides of his head. A thin man himself, he wears thin-framed, rectangular glasses over narrow, hazel eyes. But when he speaks, his native Louisianan drawl changes everything. His voice is soft and relaxed and gallant. He transforms from a "suit" into the cliché of some affable country lawyer from the Bayou. Opponents have fallen for that act before; to their lasting regret. But now he's courtly.

"Valerie, it *is* a pleasure to meet you. I've heard a great many lovely things about you and your times with Lori. Welcome to Louisiana… Now… shall we get down to business?"

Sam sits and interlaces the fingers of his hands into a bunch before him on the table.

"Valerie, Roy has told me the basics of your case. I shall want to ask you a great many questions this afternoon… But before we start, there is one thing I'd like you to know: we never take a case that we don't expect to win."

At afternoon's end, Sam clears his throat and smiles. "We would like to represent you, Valerie. You will not pay us anything unless we win. We will pay all expenses until then."

Now Valerie shakes her head and marvels at the odyssey that so far has spanned four years' of travel, investigations, documentation, depositions, paper wars and now, this trial. The judge's voice breaks into her reveries.

"Mr. Payne, would you please call your first witness?"

"Your Honor I'd like to call Ms. Rita Mohsin to the stand."

***

The previous evening, Roy takes time away from his trial rehearsals—he has a mock podium in his room, from which he questions imaginary witnesses—to visit with his clients in their room.

The entire plaintiff's entourage—John, Valerie, Roy, Roy's daughter, Julie, who is a lawyer with the firm, Sam, and their chief secretary, a woman named Starla—camps in The Adolphus Hotel, a block from the courthouse.

The Adolphus, built by St. Louis beer baron Adolphus Busch in 1912, bills itself as the flagship of:

"... the Gilded Age of Glamour... Style, elegance and grandeur blend together in 21 stories of unabashed beaux arts splendor that critics quickly named 'the most beautiful building west of Venice.'... Throughout its history, luminaries such as Queen Elizabeth II, the Vanderbilts, Oscar de la Renta, Donald Trump, U2 and Babe Ruth have chosen The Adolphus as their Dallas home-away-from-home. They are drawn by its magic and majesty and charmed by its warm and gracious staff, who unfurl the red carpet for all who enter its gilded doors. This is hospitality of a by-gone age, tailored to individual tastes and desires. The Adolphus will add a touch of European sophistication to your Lone Star visit."

In Valerie's opinion, the glamour of the place fades fast when she discovers that their room has no hot water. When they mention this to the staff they are told, "Hey, it's an old hotel. It takes a lot of time for hot water to make its way around... Or maybe it's 'cause the boiler is at the opposite end of this place from your room. By the time other people take their showers in the mornings, it just runs out." Great. The fact is, it's just an old hotel.

Roy knocks on their door around 8 p.m. Though Valerie is already in her pajamas, she's up, as is John, and they welcome him in. He sits on the edge of the bed.

"I just thought you might want to hear what we're planning for tomorrow."

"All ears," John and Valerie say at the same time.

"Well... I'm going to call Rita Mohsin as our first witness. She lied during her deposition. I mean outrageous, incredible lies. I want to pin down that testimony right away and get the jury on our side—right from the start—by getting them to see Mohsin as a liar. By extension it should taint the other side. Right after that I'll bring on our eyewitness from the plane. Their direct contradictions of Mohsin should seal the deal. Any questions so far?"

"Yes," Valerie says. "Who's that blonde woman sitting with the defense? She's been giving me bad looks the whole time—like she'd kill me if she had the chance."

"Ha. She's one of The Federation's VPs. She's a b— Well… she is as she appears."

"A bitch." Valerie concludes. She lightens suddenly.

"So we're good?" she says.

"Well, good for now," Roy cautions. "Our biggest challenge is this: The defense isn't going to deny that you're injured *now*; they don't have to. You were injured originally in 2000. The defense is going to say that you've been this way all along. We have to show that, yes, you were injured, but that you came back, you recovered and were injured again—by them. That's a big hill for us to climb."

Valerie's face sags, betraying her insecurity. Roy takes her hand.

"Don't worry. We have a lot of things going for us… One of the best is that those guys never took this case seriously. They've dropped the ball several times over this whole process… And now they're going to pay for their arrogance."

***

"Good morning," Roy says. "Would you please state your name for the record?"

"Rita Mohsin."

Mohsin, her face passive and inscrutable, takes the stand and swears to God that she will tell the truth, the whole truth and nothing but the truth.

Roy emphasizes the fact that she's taken an oath and faces perjury charges if she does not tell the truth. He lets that soak in and then gets down to business by asking about the flight. His first thrust will be to establish that she traveled on behalf of her employer—a key fact when it comes to The Federation's liability.

"Where were you going at that time?"

"Boston, Massachusetts."

"What were you going there for?"

"Work."

"What event was that?"

"It was for a project, and my role was to demonstrate an application."

"So it was not a conference or a seminar?"

"No."

"Were you required to go to Boston as part of your job to make this demonstration?"

"Yes."

"You were required to travel on the weekend?"

"Yes."

"How did you book your travel?"

"We are required to go through the company's travel agent."

"Would you have paid for it, or would the Federation?"

"Federation."

Roy nods then walks in a small circle before moving into the facts of the accident. He takes a breath.

"Describe for me what happened when you were putting your bag into the overhead bin."

"I pushed the handle down on my luggage. I lifted it into the cabin. But my fingers twisted and slipped, and the luggage ended up on the airplane ground. I noticed I had—that is, the bag had brushed Ms. Valerie's head. So I immediately apologized. Ms. Jeanne got up immediately and helped me put the luggage into the cabin."

"So the bag fell all the way to the floor?"

"It brushed Ms. Valerie's hair, and I grasped it; and I rested it on the airplane floor."

"Did the bag fall all the way to the floor, or did you set it down?"

"It did not fall. I set it down. I grasped the—I turned my hand and got a good grasp on it, and then I rested it on the airplane ground."

"Are you saying that both of your hands remained on the bag at all times?"

"Yes. But my right hand was a little bit twisted, but I had my two hands on it as it slid; and I grasped it and laid it down."

"Did you talk to Valerie at any point?"

"Yes. I asked her if she was okay, and do I need to call the hostess?"

"And why did you ask that?"

"Just out of courtesy."

"Did you think that your bag had struck her?"

"No. I believe it just brushed her hair."

"Not her head, just her hair?"

"Yes."

"And yet you asked her if she was all right and if she needed assistance?"

"Yes."

"And why would you ask that if you thought that you had just touched her hair?"

"I don't know. I just asked."

"And did she say anything in response?"

"She said, 'I'm fine.'"

"Did you *ever* hear her say anything else during the rest of that flight?"

"No."

"You said the bag just brushed her hair. How do you know it didn't hit her head?"

"I just felt the contact very—barely touching the hair."

"So you could tell that it hit something?"

"I don't know."

"You felt the contact, you said?"

"I felt the contact."

"Did you observe, during that flight, that she was in pain?"

"No."

"Did American Airlines ever ask you to give a statement?"

"No."

"Did they request your permission to release their report to Valerie?"

"Yes. I received a letter."

"Did you give them permission?"

"No."

"Why not?"

"I didn't think of any of this at that point."

"But you told them not to release the report to Valerie?"

"Yes."

"Did you think it was your fault that your bag contacted her head?"

Here, the chief opposing counsel, a Mr. Demerit, rises and calls out, "Objection to form!" but his client is already answering.

"It was an accident. It was not intentional."

"Do you think accidents are nobody's fault?"

"It was not intentional."

"I'm not asking whether you *intended* for your bag to hit her. I'm asking: Do you believe it was your responsibility, your fault, that the bag hit her?"

"Objection: form!"

Again, she answers before a ruling comes along.

"I don't know," she says.

Roy smiles. "If someone accidentally runs their car into the back of your car, do you think they're responsible for that?"

"I would think so."

"Is that because you think they intended it?"

"No."

"So they're responsible even though they didn't intend it?"

"In this regards."

"Are you responsible even though you didn't intend that your bag hit her head?"

"Objection!"

Judge Kaplan waves for Demerit to sit. "Answer please," he says calmly.

"Then I would say yes."

"Did you ever check back with Valerie at the end of that flight or at any other time to see how she was?"

"Yes."

"What did she say?"

"Before I left the airplane, I took my luggage down; and I apologized again and said thank you and left the airplane."

"Do you remember a little earlier in your testimony today I asked you if you ever spoke with Valerie again after the first time when the bag fell on her; and you told me you never spoke to her again."

"I spoke to her a total of three times."

"I see. Perhaps you'd forgotten. So, tell me about those three times."

"One was when the bag slipped. The second was during the flight when I got up and—

"What did you say to her then?"

"Are you okay. I'm sorry. Are you okay?"

"And why did you ask her that?"

"Just courtesy… and once on my way back from the bathroom."

"You thought that you had only brushed her hair and yet you asked her again if she was okay?"

"Yes."

"Okay, and then you spoke with her again?"

"Yes."

"And what did you say?"

"'I'm sorry,' again, and 'I hope you're okay,' and I left.

"And that's all because you thought you had merely *brushed* her hair?'"

"Yeah."

"Thank you."

The defense does not cross-examine.

As soon as Mohsin steps down. Roy says, "Your Honor, our next witnesses will appear on the video screen—their testimonies and cross-examinations having been recorded under oath and admitted as evidence here."

"Proceed."

"This first deposition is that of a Mr. Greg Sconce."

What the jury doesn't know is that the video depositions had been done long before the defense ever took the case seriously. Rather than send their own lawyers across the country to depose and cross-examine Roy's witnesses, they'd farmed it out to surrogate local lawyers. They hadn't realized the error of their ways until too late when one of their associates signed away their right to challenge.

The courtroom lights dim a little and a video projects upon a large screen visible to the jury. Before them, on the screen, a balding, hefty man, with a fringe of white hair, who appears to be in his late fifties, sits at a table, with a serious look on his face. Roy's voice, off-camera, asks the man his name and business address, then:

"Do you remember an American Airlines flight from DFW to Boston about this time last year? In January of '07? When a bag fell on a woman passenger?"

"Yes I do."

"Had you ever seen that woman passenger before that day or since that day?"

"No. I have not."

"I'm going to call her Valerie for simplicity. Would that be all right?"

"That would be fine."

"When did you first see Valerie that day?"

"She boarded onto the aircraft prior to me. I walked past her. She was a seat or two up on the right hand side to my seat."

"Did you see her when they were getting her onboard?

"No sir, I did not."

"You walked past her then and sat down in your seat?"

"Yes."

"What next drew your attention to her?"

"Watching passengers as they were coming toward me, I noticed her—frail looking."

"The woman who had the suitcase that hit Valerie—I'm going to call her Ms. Mohsin for simplicity sake—when did you first notice Ms. Mohsin?"

"She approached Valerie's area. She was dragging a suitcase behind her. She picked it up, like this…" Here Sconce pantomimes the action of someone hoisting a heavy weight upward.

"And lifted it over her head and put it about half way into the overhead compartment and without further ado, just looked away and walked away. She got to her seat—one seat behind Valerie—and the suitcase teetered and fell and hit Valerie in the head."

"As you recall it, did her hands stay on the bag, or when she turned, did she let go of the bag?"

"She put the bag up very nonchalant. Carelessly. The bag was not stable when she walked away."

Here the opposing attorney's video voice says casually, "Object to the response."

Roy continues. "Did you see the bag make contact with Valerie?"

"Yes, I did. The bag fell, hit her in the head."

"If Ms. Mohsin has stated that her bag simply brushed Valerie's hair, and did not hit her head, would you agree with that?"

"No sir, I would not."

"Could you tell whether the bag appeared to strike her with force?"

Again the opposing attorney's voice: "Object to form."

Sconce goes on. "It hit her in the head and the bag weighs, what? 30 to 40 pounds?"

"I'm going to show you a photograph of Ms. Mohsin at her deposition along with the bag she produced at that deposition and testified was the one she had on that date and ask you if that appears to you to be the bag that you remember, or of the same size."

Sconce takes the photograph and examines it carefully.

"Actually, this one in the picture looks quite a bit smaller."

"After the bag struck Valerie, what reaction do you recall Ms. Mohsin having after that?"

"Absolutely none. She sat in her chair, picked up a magazine and could care less."

"Object to the response."

"Do you recall at any time during that flight, did Ms. Mohsin check on Valerie or help her in any way?"

"She did not offer any help, assistance or question."

"From where you were seated, were you able to see Valerie and Ms. Mohsin during the flight?"

"Yes. I could clearly see them."

"After the bag struck Valerie, what did you do?"

"I called the flight attendant. Hit the button overhead, and they came up immediately."

"What did you describe to the flight attendants when they came up?"

"They asked if anybody witnessed it. And I told them what I'd seen."

"Do you recall if there was another woman who came up and gave her name?"

"Yes, sir. I don't recall the name, but she sat behind me, one row back."

"After you called the flight attendants, did they offer assistance to Valerie?"

"Yes, they did."

"Do you recall what they may have done for her?"

"I do not."

"Do you remember whether Valerie appeared to be in any distress or pain as the flight went on?"

"She appeared to be in distress and pain at the time of the incident."

"Can you describe what you saw about her that led you to that conclusion about her pain?"

"Well, her head was cut and bleeding. She was holding it and shaking and tears were coming out of her eyes. And a shaky voice."

"I have no further questions," Roy says and turns the questioning over to the defendant's counsel.

"Mr. Sconce, let me ask you, about how much time elapsed between the time Ms. Mohsin put the bag in the compartment and it fell?

"Just a couple of seconds."

"And you recall had Ms. Mohsin returned to her seat when the bag fell?"

"Ms. Mohsin had not reached her seat when the bag fell. She placed it up. It teetered. She whipped around behind. She was still standing as it fell. Then she took her seat, then pulled out a magazine."

"Do you know if she realized it had fallen?"

"Oh, she looked up."

"Are you certain the bag hit Valerie in the head and not the seat-back?"

"I saw it hit her. My wife said, 'Oh my God.'"

There's a silent pause on the video until the defense attorney speaks again.

"Um… did you hear Valerie speak at any time subsequent to the accident?"

"Yes. The flight attendants asked her if she was okay and she said, 'No, I'm hurt.'"

The next video is the testimony of a Ms. McMunn who sat nearby. The testimony mirrors that of Mr. Sconce, but is even more emphatic when it comes to the size of the luggage.

Roy's voice: "I'm going to show you a photograph of Ms. Mohsin at her deposition with the bag that *she* says she had that day and ask you if it looks like the bag that you saw strike Valerie."

The jury watches McMunn examine the photo.

"It was a much larger bag than that, I'm sure," she says.

Roy then produces the actual bag that Mohsin claimed as hers at the time, and puts it in front of the camera.

"Does this look like the bag that you recall hitting Valerie?"

"No. It was a *much* larger bag."

"Just one more thing," Roy says. "When everyone got off the plane, do you recall whether Ms. Mohsin stopped to check on Valerie?"

"I remember that because I was so astounded that somebody wouldn't be concerned. I mean, the bag hit her with such an impact, and I was so astounded that someone wouldn't see if she was okay."

The video ends. The lights come up. The defense cannot cross examine the video: too late for that. Roy walks back to his table.

***

When not in court, Valerie and John are confined to their hotel room—not confined to the hotel, but confined to the *room*. Which means that, though the place has three separate restaurants, Valerie and John will only get the limited selections of room service for the duration. Roy imposed the restriction because you never know what the opposition might try—a photograph which, when viewed in a certain way, makes Valerie look well; or perhaps a moment when they might accidentally bump into a juror and somehow taint the case; or… well, who knows? Just stay inside, cover all the bases.

So, for them, the week revolves around room service, trial rehearsals, court appearances and no hot water.

Valerie, wound up, doesn't sleep. Her appetite for food drops—perhaps due to the ordinary and repetitive room service fare (only eggs, hamburgers, BLTs, turkey sandwiches, and Cobb salads) or, more likely, she doesn't eat due to the tension and fear of the threatening confrontation that is a trial.

After a dinner of yet another Cobb salad, there's a knock on the door, which John answers. In the doorway is Roy and Dr. Indira Lanig, Valerie's long-time spinal cord injury specialist from Denver.

Dr. Lanig has jet-black hair, is slender and is exotically pretty. She smiles. "Hello John. May we come in?"

"Of course. Come, come."

They enter. The remarkable thing about Dr. Lanig being in the room—or in Dallas at all—is that expert medical witnesses rarely, if ever, attend out-of-town trials. The normal process is for them to sit for a deposition in their hometowns and be done with it. But once again, there's been something about Valerie—perhaps it's her cheery spirit, or her relentless determination—that compels the doctor to make a special

196

trip to appear in court, to testify in person on her patient's behalf.

"How are you holding up?" she asks Valerie, who smiles and nods.

"Pretty good. All things considered, you know."

Roy pulls up a chair for Dr. Lanig and sits with her at a table.

"Dr. Lanig just wanted to come by tonight and see you. I'm putting her on the stand tomorrow and we'll be going over some material for about an hour tonight."

"Thank you so much for coming," Valerie says.

"I feel very strongly about this," Dr. Lanig smiles.

"So, what happens tomorrow?" John asks.

"Tomorrow, Dr. Lanig will explain to the jury a number of things, but most important is that she will explain, medically, that Valerie was recovering from her initial injury. She'll explain what a 'tethered' spinal cord is; that Valerie had a tethered spinal cord; that the impact from the suitcase caused Valerie's tethered cord to stretch, which directly caused all the setbacks she's suffering."

Valerie exhales sharply. "Wow. Will they understand all that?"

"It's complicated—that's our problem. But I believe so," Roy says. "I'm going to take it slowly, methodically. We're going to pre-empt the defense's positions. It's important that the jury understand what happened medically. All the defense needs to do is shed doubt, make the jury think that maybe something else caused your setback, or that you've been like this all along... But don't worry. It will go fine."

Roy and Dr. Lanig rise and say their goodnights.

"Oh, one more thing," Roy adds. "You should stay here tomorrow. I don't want you in the courtroom for this."

After her doctor and lawyer leave, Valerie tries to sleep. But a thousand what-ifs flood her mind and she doesn't sleep a wink.

***

"Your Honor, I'd like to call Dr. Indira Lanig to testify."

Dr. Lanig is brought into the courtroom. She wears a grey business suit/skirt ensemble and walks toward the dock with a sure step. Her beauty—possibly distracting—is trumped by an all-business demeanor. She does not even glance at the defense table, otherwise she would see the sneer sent her way by The Federation's blonde VP.

After she takes the stand and is sworn in, Roy approaches.

"Good morning, Dr. Lanig. Would you please give us your business address?"

"Of course. It is 3425 South Clarkson, Englewood, Colorado."

"And that is at Craig Hospital?"

"Correct."

"I'm going to ask you to give us your background so the jury will know something about you."

Through questioning, Dr. Lanig's credentials are established: a medical degree from Baylor, residency in physical medicine and rehabilitation, chief of the spinal cord injury unit at Houston's VA Hospital, board certified in both physical medicine/rehabilitation and spinal cord injury medicine, chief of the spinal cord injury facility at the Baylor College of Medicine in Houston and at Craig Hospital in Denver; she is published in textbooks on the subject of spinal cord injury and is involved in ongoing research on spinal cord injuries at Craig. Roy asks that the court accept her as an expert witness.

Next he establishes the basics: Dr. Lanig first treated Valerie in Denver after she was released from the Baylor Rehabilitation Hospital in Dallas after her initial injury. They review the nature of Valerie's first injury and that Dr. Lanig had been Valerie's spinal cord injury-treating physician since then except for when Valerie lived in Boston.

"Over the course of the eleven years that you've been involved with Valerie, have you observed that she's worked hard at helping her own recovery?"

"Yes."

"Objection, form." Demerit stands up.

"All right," Roy says. "I'll rephr—"

"I can tell you what my objection is if you want," the counsel interrupts again. "I don't think she's been seeing this patient for eleven years, so I think that's a mischaracterization."

Judge Kaplan says nothing, but raises an eyebrow and points a finger toward Demerit, who stops speaking and sits back down.

"I'll rephrase the question," Roy replies, then turns again to the physician. "Have you been seeing Valerie over a course of about eleven years?"

"Approximately eleven years. Yes."

"Okay. During that time, have you observed that she's worked hard at helping her own recovery?"

"She's always been highly motivated."

"And you last saw Valerie before her move to Boston back in 2004; is that right?

"Yes."

"Do you remember generally what her level of function was as far as walking and signing and working?"

"At that time, she was ambulatory. She was able to have bipedal mobility. She didn't have a normal walking pattern. It was wobbly and a bit unsteady, slow—but she could walk. She was also able to use sign language."

"And was she working at that time as you recall?"

"I believe she was working and then going to take another position in Boston."

"When Valerie moved to Boston, her care was transferred to a Dr. Kevin O'Connor. Are you familiar with him?"

"Yes."

"Does Spaulding Rehabilitation Hospital where Dr. O'Connor practices have a good reputation within the spinal cord injury community?"

"Dr. O'Connor does."

"And is he known to you to be a spinal cord injury specialist?"

"Yes."

"You next saw Valerie when she moved back to Denver in 2007. Is that right?"

"Correct."

"What history on her did you receive at that time?"

"Let me look at my notes... She gave me a brief update on how things had unfolded while she was in Boston. She was using a one-sided cane until she sprained an ankle, and then she was using bilateral crutches. And then she related that in January of that year, she had some luggage from an overhead bin land on her head; and she had transient 'zingers,' which are like an electrical body jolt, and paralysis—transient paralysis. And she described a large lump at the base of her neck, and she was having smoldering pain between her shoulder blades that was still problematic."

"And was she experiencing a deterioration in her level of function at the time you saw her in June of '07 from what she had had before?"

"Yes. Her function wasn't what it was in 2006."

"Over the last 20 plus years, you've treated hundreds if not a thousand or more spinal cord injury patients? Is that fair to say?"

"Probably."

"And you expect to see fluctuations in their level of function as they deal with different ailments, different problems? Is that fair to say?"

"No. People are fairly stable. They may have good days and bad days. But in terms of wide fluctuations, you typically don't see that."

"And during the years that you had seen Valerie before 2007, had her level of function been fairly stable?"

"It *had* been fairly stable."

Roy anticipates that, later, the opposition will try to discredit anything Valerie told her doctor following the accident. To preempt that move, he asks about how, exactly and objectively, Dr. Lanig can say that Valerie's abilities deteriorated—that the doctor is not simply relying on Valerie's word. The physician describes, in detail, the hospital's sensory and motor testing procedures—a standardized way of measuring levels of sensation (using pinpricks to map pain levels around the body) and testing muscle strength.

She produces maps of Valerie's body reactions to the pinpricks.

Roy asks, "And you consider these to be *objective* tests, not just depending on the accuracy of the patient, but things that you can measure and monitor?"

"Correct. There's actually a comment line where the therapist can document if there's anything that doesn't seem straightforward."

"And based on your testing and your records regarding Valerie, did she experience a marked decrease in her neurological functioning in 2007 and 2008 after that suitcase accident in January of 2007?"

"Based on our records, she had changed fairly dramatically in terms of sensation as well as strength. When we looked at the motor testing, at the fine muscles in her hands, they had significantly decreased and stiffened with her spasticity and so she wasn't able to be bilingual anymore with signing. As her fingers got weaker, she couldn't use sign language."

"Now, based on the hundreds of spinal cord injury patients you've treated, when you have a second injury like a blow to the head from the suitcase that Valerie had, do you often see a rapid deterioration of neurological function?"

"When there is a rapid acceleration-deceleration type of injury, it can stretch the spinal cord. The function starts deteriorating from that. Like with Valerie, when you've got scarring around the zone of injury, you can see a very rapid—well, rapid in our world—deterioration in function. It can be immediate or it can extend over several months where a person thinks, 'Well, maybe I'm just having a bad day,' and then more, and more bad days start adding up and they realize, 'Oh, wait a minute. I am clearly changing.'"

"Now, based on the relatively stable functioning that Valerie had during the years before the suitcase blow, could she have continued in her steady state indefinitely had it not been for this suitcase event?

"She could have continued indefinitely."

***

Back at the hotel, Valerie waits for John who has made a brief prison break in search of some thin crust pizza down the street. He returns with an aromatic, grease-stained box.

"Oh, heaven." Valerie grins.

They dig in and say nothing until both have consumed two slices each. Then John says, "I wonder how it's going."

"It's going fine," Valerie says. "Everything's fine."

***

Roy looks from Dr. Lanig to the jury. The juror's faces betray nothing—except the fact that none of them has fallen asleep. He takes it as a good sign. He looks back toward the witness.

"Now, doctor, can you explain to the jury what tethering is?"

Dr. Lanig explains that tethering of the spinal cord is a condition in which the spinal cord becomes attached to the spinal column via surrounding structures. Normally, the spinal cord hangs loose in the canal. A tethered cord does not move. If a tethered cord is suddenly pulled or stretched, it can reduce blood flow to the spinal nerves and cause damage to the spinal cord itself. If such a situation is left untreated, it can lead to progressive, permanent spinal cord damage.

Roy continues. "Is someone with a tethered spinal cord especially vulnerable to injury from a blow like the suitcase accident?"

"Yes. It's like if you have an extensive scar on your skin, that scar oftentimes isn't as supple as your normal skin and so it may crack more easily or tear open more easily because it doesn't have the flexibility, the tensile strength that normal skin does. So a tethered cord doesn't have the play that an untethered cord does."

"And when there's a blow to the head which causes the cord to move up and down rapidly within the canal, it is stretched or damaged by those tethering scars?"

"Yes. There's a yanking."

"Okay. Now, is there a surgery designed to correct this tethering?"

"Yes."

"And is Craig Hospital, one of the leading hospitals for that kind of surgery?"

"Yes. Dr. Falci is internationally recognized for his expertise in that area."

"Did you refer Valerie to him for considering having that surgery?"

"Yes, based on her history, her new complaints, and then the changes that we saw on sensory and motor testing, I referred her to Dr. Falci and she ultimately had surgery in 2008."

"Is one of the risks that patients are told about in advance of this surgery complete paralysis?"

"Yes."

"That's something that they're warned could happen if it's not successful?"

"Correct. And I also warn them that when they come out of surgery, they are going to swear that something went wrong because they are going to be in excruciating pain. When people wake up, they feel like they're laying on a jagged rock. It's just not pretty."

"Did the blow to the head that Valerie had in January of '07 more probably than not cause the need for Valerie to have this untethering surgery in May?"

"Yes."

"Did you check on Valerie in the hospital after her surgery?"

"Yes."

"How was she doing when you first saw her after the surgery?"

"Not well. The nurse on duty told me that Valerie was having a fair amount of head pain and her pain medicines weren't quite working. So I walked into Valerie's room. She was holding her head and just sobbing silently because she was in so much pain. And I just looked at her. I remember thinking, 'Ooh, this is really bad, you know, patient holding head before you even walk into the room.' Valerie's pain was of a magnitude that we were worried might be completely out of control. We had to take her down to radiology, make sure she wasn't leaking spinal fluid... She was leaking, so we put in an extra suture, and I aggressively covered her with pain medicines to get her through the next 48 hours."

"Okay. Do you believe that more probably than not Valerie's current level of function is about as good as it's going to get?"

"Looking at May through August, it's probably as good as it's going to get in terms of her day-to-day function. We're going to try to dampen out some of her spasticity a little bit more, but I don't think she's going to get much stronger."

And this is why Roy kept Valerie away from the courtroom today: he doesn't want her to hear any negative prognoses. A positive attitude has sustained and motivated Valerie through everything and Roy will be damned if he's going to undo that for the sake of a trial. So Valerie doesn't hear him ask the doctor:

"More probably than not, do you believe that her use of her hands in terms of sign language is about as good as that's going to get?"

"Considering where she was before and where she is now, it's probably as good as it's going to get unless I can dampen out her spasticity a little bit so she doesn't have to fight quite as much."

"Do you think she's likely to ever recover the kind of fluency with sign language that she had before this January of 2007 event?"

"It's unlikely."

"Do you believe that Valerie will likely, meaning more probably than not, have to have a second untethering surgery?"

"Based on clinical experience, I suspect we're going to be faced with that sometime in the future."

"And would a second untethering surgery be similar to the one that you've described earlier?"

"Yes."

"And could Valerie, based on where she was in 2006, have gone on indefinitely without needing untethering surgery but for that suitcase accident?"

"She could have gone on indefinitely without needing that surgery."

"Thank you, Doctor. That's all the questions I have."

The defense counsel rises and approaches the

witness.

"Doctor, my name is David Demerit; and I represent the defendant in this lawsuit. Forgive me if I go back over some things... *I* haven't had an opportunity to talk with you until today; is that correct?"

"Correct."

"I assume you've talked with *Ms. Daniell's* attorney before today?"

"Correct."

"The two of you went over the things that he was going to discuss with you here at the trial?"

"Broadly."

"Okay... Broadly enough that you were able to bring some illustrations and things of that nature with you, correct?

"Cor—."

"...and be prepared for some of the questions that he may or may not ask you, correct?"

"I usually bring visual aids."

"Is that a yes or a no to my question? You weren't prepared for the questions he was going to ask you?

"I was fairly prepared for them."

"Okay. Because you had a discussion with him beforehand?"

"His questions were pretty regular."

"All right. Have you had any discussion with Ms. Daniell about this lawsuit and your testimony here today?"

"No. Only that she was going to file a case."

"And so the jury can understand, you're a treating physician of hers, correct? And you're here because they've asked you to come here. You don't consider yourself an advocate in this case, I assume; correct?"

"Correct."

"Okay. Well, I assume you're getting paid for your time?"

"I hope so."

"All right. Have you worked out an arrangement for that?"

"My office takes care of that."

"Okay. But you believe that you're being paid by Ms. Daniell to be here today, correct?"

"I might end up being paid by *you*."

A spectator laughs.

The judge glares at the man and says threateningly: "Order."

Demerit pauses, and smoothes the front of his suit.

"Well, I can assure you, you're not being paid by me."

The doctor replies, "We'll see, I suppose."

This time the same spectator who had laughed earlier—pushes his face down inside the crown of his cowboy hat and suppresses another laugh.

Demerit keeps his eyes fixed on the doctor, then changes the subject.

"You can obviously understand the difficulty in this case is that there's a significant injury in 2000, and you're now assessing how much change has occurred as of an event in 2007 with a—everybody would agree—fragile patient at that time; correct?"

"*Stably* fragile."

"Stably fragile when you last saw her in 2003?"

Here, Roy interjects. "I believe 2004 is the—"

Demerit wheels around. "I didn't ask for your testimony, Roy." He turns back to Dr. Lanig.

"Do you recall the last time you saw her? I asked you and you said you didn't know because it's not in the chart?"

"If the records show that it was '04, then that was the last time I saw her before summer '07."

"All right. So you would agree with me, though, the best you can say is she was stable the last time you saw her?"

"Correct."

"You don't know what's happened to Ms. Daniell from the time you saw her until she returned in the summer of 2007, correct?"

"Except for what she related to us."

"Exactly. And you have to rely on her to tell you everything that happened to her so that you can make an appropriate diagnosis, correct?"

"Correct."

"And if she had several accidents or several falls, you would then have to take that into consideration as to a potential cause... or does that even matter to you?"

Lanig takes a moment to let the implied insult fade from her thoughts.

"What's important is for the patient to give me as much information as possible, so that I can connect the dots. So I will ask about falls. I will ask for what happened after such and such. How are things different? And they share information accordingly."

"Okay. Let me talk to you a little bit about Ms. Daniell when she first presented to you back in, I think, 2001. When did you see her and what was her prognosis at that time?"

"Let me get my laptop because—"

"Because you don't recall at this time?"

Roy interrupts. "Mr. Demerit, you and I both have the records. I'm happy to hand Dr. Lanig the records from her initial visit in November of 2000 if that would help."

The lawyer again spins around and this time nearly shouts.

"I would appreciate it if you'd quit interrupting my questioning. If she doesn't have the records in front of her, she brought what she chose to bring with her so that she could testify for you. If you want to correct me from

2001 to November of 2000, then that's fine. I'd prefer that I'm allowed to ask her questions, and then you can come back on direct and correct if you think there's a problem."

Roy shrugs. "Just offering the records if you thought it'd be helpful."

"I don't need—the problem—I don't think she has the entire record in front of her."

Dr. Lanig says, "I can get the entire record on laptop."

"The jury understands that she doesn't have the record."

"Gentlemen!"

It's Judge Kaplan. "That will be enough… Mr. Payne, don't interrupt Mr. Demerit, again… Mr. Demerit, get on with it. If you want the information, she can provide it for you. If you don't then just move on."

Demerit shrugs and turns back to the witness. "You're familiar with patients who undergo spinal cord surgery are at a higher risk to come back and have subsequent surgeries as a result of the surgical intervention itself, correct?"

"Not necessarily."

Demerit swallows hard, goes to his table and drinks water. He wears the look of a man losing ground.

"Okay," he says. "It's your testimony that the symptoms from the tethering was a result of some traumatic incident; correct? It's the only explanation given to you by your patient—the luggage on the head?"

"Correct."

"But, obviously, you weren't present and didn't examine her or give her an MRI immediately after this event."

"No. As I understand it from the record, that examination was done in Boston just 18 hours after the event."

And now Demerit, unable to shake the witness, inadvertently begins to make his opponents' case.

"Okay. Tethering in her spine would have to be present for another traumatic event to have caused her new symptoms, correct?"

"Correct."

"What type of instantaneous symptoms would result from that type of injury?"

"Exactly the ones she described immediately after the event and in the weeks that followed."

"And as I understand what you're telling me is that Ms. Daniell conveyed that type of feeling to you as occurring in January of 2007 after this event?"

"Correct."

"But then let's just assume then that since the time you started treating her in November of 2000 until today, the only type of zinger she's ever had was as a result of this event on the plane?"

"The only abrupt type of zinger and concurrent change in strength was then."

"All right. Now you've somewhat changed the analysis, so I want to go back over—"

"No. I haven't"

"So you're saying that she's not had any zingers with an abrupt strength change other than this one event that she's told you about?"

"In so far as I can recall from looking through her chart."

"Okay. What if she had a series of falls over a three- or four-year period of time? Is it important that you identify the single event that caused the symptoms?"

Lanig sighs.

"I'm trying to figure out how best to connect a clinical reality to your hypothetical one."

"You mean you're not aware of other falls is what you're saying?"

"Not aware of *major* falls. But patients fall. That's why we teach them how to get up off the floor and teach them how to do controlled falls and not have major splats."

"And why is that?"

"Broken bones aren't fun."

Before anyone can laugh, the judge casts a warning gaze across the room. The cowboy in the gallery rises, chuckling and shaking his head as he voluntarily leaves the courtroom.

Demerit tries a grin. "Okay. Dr. Lanig, I understand your position here. You want to help Ms. Daniell. I understand—"

"No. I'm just trying to explain medicine to you."

"What you're saying is that the only information you have or only explainable reason you have for those symptoms is the fall from the luggage, correct?"

"Correct. Because most people with a traumatic spinal cord injury are tethered, but very few are symptomatic."

At this point, Roy leans over to his grinning partner and whispers, "Criminey. He's digging his own grave."

Sam nods. "Yup."

Too late, the counsel abandons his line of questioning and goes a different route.

"Have you ever had patients involved in lawsuits before?"

"Yes."

"Okay. Does it in any way affect the way you treat those patients?"

"Not really."

"Do you believe that those patients have some incentive to report symptoms that might not otherwise be directly involved with the litigation event?"

"The catastrophic injury by itself is usually

incentive enough."

The attorney goes over the same ground over and over, for another hour, but finds no way to snare Dr. Lanig. When several jury members begin to fidget, he cuts his losses.

"I think that's all the questions I have. Thank you."

At this point, Roy rises again.

"I have just a couple more questions, Dr. Lanig, and I promise I'll be brief... Doctor, Mr. Demerit asked you about the charge for your time in giving this testimony. Is it true that the clinic that you're with has a charge for your time for every testimony that you give?"

"Correct. They have a schedule."

"And there's a schedule for each of the doctors in the clinic?"

"We actually all use the same schedule."

"So there's nothing different about Valerie Daniell's case from any other case where you give testimony. There's always a charge?"

"Correct."

"Is there anything unusual in your practice about meeting with the patient's lawyer before the testimony when they're about to take your testimony?"

"I usually meet with the lawyer before."

"And was there anything different about your meeting with me and your meeting with a lawyer for any other patient that you would give testimony on?"

"No."

"I'm going to read to you the history that Dr. Michael Bean, her primary care physician in Boston, recorded about *within 24 hours of the accident*. And I'll show it to you in a moment and ask you if it's consistent with what you were told by Valerie when you first saw her. Dr. Bean recorded:

"'Suitcase fell on her head yesterday, hurt like hell,

felt like her whole spine was crushed, felt numbness and tingling in the hands. Sitting there through the flight, started getting neck pain radiating down the back, got up and walked around to keep things moving, went home and felt back and neck tightness, called the on-call doc, referred here. This a.m. awoke with diffuse ache, feels like she's tight, feels the numbness and tingling in her fingers still. When she walks, feels tight. The numbness and tingling is definitely new.'"

Roy hands the doctor the report, which she reads.

"Is that consistent with what Valerie told you when you first saw her after the accident in June of '07?"

"Yes."

"And does that reinforce the clinical findings and the diagnosis that you made that this event was the trauma that unmasked the tethering and created these symptoms that led to the surgery?"

"Yes."

"Okay. The yank on the spinal cord, when it's tethered, damages the spinal cord which is that bundle of nerves itself, doesn't it?"

"Correct."

"And untethering it, cutting away all that scar tissue, doesn't make the damage to the nerves in the spinal cord go away or get better; does it?

"Correct. Permanently injured cells won't recover."

The court takes a recess and the spectators and clerks file out. Roy and Sam pack their papers; their staff begins to load their mountain of files onto collapsible hand-trucks. Mr. Demerit wanders over to Roy.

"You must have worked with her for weeks," he says.

Roy ignores him and continues packing.

"All right, here it is: let's quit this nonsense now.

We'll offer you $500,000."

Roy looks over to Sam, who does not look up, but does smile.

"I'm obligated to take your offer to my client," Roy says. "But don't get your hopes up."

***

That evening, before seeing Valerie and John, Roy holds a staff conference in the "war room" the living room portion of Sam's suite. The sofas and most of the room's chairs are pushed back against the walls. One table remains in the center, amid boxes of files, computers, a fax machine, and papers arranged in heaps like money stacks in a Vegas counting room.

"They've offered us $500,000 to settle," Roy tells the group.

"Take it," says Julie, his daughter, who is in her early years of practicing law.

"Why do you say that?" Roy asks—more interested in her reasoning than in making any point himself.

"This case is risky. The medicine part was too complicated for a jury to grasp. I don't know if you made it with them today. I watched them—they're impossible to read. We've spent tons on this case. Let's just get something and go."

"Relax," Sam says in a voice that is so soothing and calm itself that Julie seems to release about as fast as a deflated balloon. "I'd advise our clients to reject this offer… Trust me on this."

Julie nods okay. Sam has, after all, seen hundreds of these cases; one way or another she'll learn something important from all this.

Roy visits Valerie and John in their room and sits

at its main table, which now is strewn with room service debris that include an untouched half of a turkey sandwich.

"Have something to eat," Valerie says. "You probably skipped lunch and everything else."

"What about you?"

"I'm done. Not very hungry."

"All right. Don't mind if I do."

Roy devours the sandwich in seconds.

"Thanks." He dabs at his mouth with a used napkin. "So the reason I'm here again—other than I miss you two—is to let you know they've offered you $500,000 to settle the case. My advice is to turn them down."

John looks at Valerie.

"I don't want you to lose money on this, Roy," Valerie says. "Would $500,000 cover what you've spent so far?"

Roy chuckles. "That's not a basis for making this decision," he says. "Here's how we see it. One, that amount is not going to help you much. Two, they made the offer because they're beginning to think they could lose. Three, if they're thinking that, maybe the jury is too… I advise you to tell them to go to hell… Get what you came for."

Valerie looks at John, who nods. "Okay," she says. "Tell them to go to hell."

Roy grins. "That's the spirit… Tomorrow, I'll be questioning your therapists. They'll talk about the progress you made since 2000."

"Should I be there this time?"

"Sure."

***

Once again, the jurors see videotaped testimony that, due to the defense's earlier error, is admissible and not subject to any cross-examination, other than what's already on the tape.

The jurors see John Vernon, a middle-aged man with brown, thinning hair. He appears trim and fit, though somewhat ill at ease, almost sad. He's a personal trainer at Gold's Gym and Easy Motions Senior Fitness Facility in Massachusetts where he worked with Valerie during her time there.

Roy's voice is heard.

"Do you recall the time period that you worked with Valerie?"

"We started in 2005 and I think it went on for about two years."

"Do you recall one of the Spaulding rehab therapists coming with Valerie to set her up to work with you?"

"I think we had one session with a woman from Spaulding who gave me an overview of the types of exercises we'd do with Valerie."

"And what types of exercises were you to do?"

"The approach I took with Valerie was to try to strengthen her entire body. Essentially a total body workout with an emphasis on the core because, I reasoned, that is where all motion originates and my goal from the beginning was to see if we could improve her mobility and general quality of life. To do that I relied on weight training and various exercises that put her in an unstable position to allow as many muscles as possible to become involved."

"What kind of client did you find Valerie to be?"

"The aspects of her situation that come to mind most readily are her willingness to work very hard, not to get discouraged, and to press forward in the face of a rather daunting situation. She had a significant injury that presented itself in several aspects: walking and general mobility. I was struck by her willingness to do whatever it took to regain some of her abilities. Her overall demeanor, her attitude of persistence and her willingness to take on some rather hard exercises."

"What kind of exercises, specifically?"

"Many of the exercises we did were on a cable machine—it allowed her to be in a standing position, creating a more difficult workout, standing in front of the machine. I also put her on a Bosu Ball, which is essentially a half-ball. I put her on that to provide an unstable base. And while she was balancing on that uneven surface, I would have her do various exercises with her extremities. Most of the cardio activities were done on a machine called a NuStep with is a recumbent bicycle that engages the lower body—it also has handle bars to exercise the upper part. We also used the stairs to gain entry into the gym, never the elevator. With me monitoring her, she made steady progress going up or down the stairs."

"What did she use to walk when she came to the workouts?"

"She would use a single cane."

"During the time you worked with her, do you recall her reporting that she'd been injured by a suitcase falling on her head on an airplane?"

"Yes. About a year and a half in our time together."

"And what effect did that have on your working with her?"

"I can't recall any workout sessions subsequent to her accident. She told me all about what had happened, but that was all after that."

"Had she been making progress during the period you did work with her?"

"She did make progress from several standpoints: the weight she was able to move increased. And I think the most interesting and salient part was that a year or so into our training, she was able to take several unaided steps, six or so, toward me without a cane or anything to hold onto at all. Completely unsupported. She was very enthused about that. She was very encouraged and I believe felt that additional improvement was likely possible."

"Thank you, Mr. Vernon… Your witness."

The defense counsel at that time introduces himself and speaks. "Mr. Vernon, have you always been a physical trainer?"

The questioning, at first tries to discredit the witness's credentials, then, failing that, scores one point: that Vernon wouldn't know what Valerie's limitations were after the suitcase accident, since he stopped seeing her then. Admittedly, it's a very small point, since long after this recording, Valerie's post-suitcase limitations have already been described by Dr. Lanig.

Next, the counselor tries to suggest bias.

"You testified about how impressed you were with Valerie's efforts," he says. "Doesn't that make you want to be an advocate for your client?"

"No."

"I mean, besides liking her as a person, she was your client, correct?"

"Yes."

"And, as a paying client, she might be the rightful recipient of your gratitude, wouldn't that be so?"

Here, for the first time, Vernon seems to relax. He chuckles softly before he speaks.

"Normally, I would charge clients $50 an hour. But I was so struck by Valerie and her situation that I did not charge her a dime."

Demerit, helpless to challenge the videotape, frowns at his seat.

Roy's next videotape witness is Beth Grill, Valerie's therapist at Spaulding. In her testimony, she describes the extensive work she and Valerie did at Spaulding.

Roy's voice: "What can you tell us about what kind of a patient Valerie was?"

"Valerie was very motivated, willing to do what was recommended to her, inspirational."

"Did you have any concerns that she might not do the work you assigned at home?"

"Not at all. She actually participated in a gym outside of therapy that has special equipment."

"If you established a spectrum of all the patients you've had, from the one's you had most trouble with getting their cooperation and attention, to the ones you had the least problems with, where would you put Valerie?"

"She would be one of the most highly motivated people that I've met."

"When she encountered adversity in the treatment you were providing, how would she react to that?"

"In a problem-solving type of way."

"Do you know of a Dr. Julie Silver, an assistant professor at Harvard Medical School?"

"I do."

"Are you familiar with a book Dr. Silver wrote by the name of *Super Healing* about patients who beat the odds with their recoveries?"

"Yes."

"Are you aware that Dr. Silver used Valerie as an example in her book?"

"I am."

Roy then asks the witness to read a report that shows Valerie graduating from a large base outdoor quad cane to a small base one. Then she reads another part of the report that shows Valerie graduating from the small quad to a standard cane and walking 250 feet with it. And a later report says she goes 500 feet.

"'Patient walked at Home Depot, Target and grocery store all day long yesterday with minimal or no fatigue... ambulated into therapy with a standard cane... Challenging her own balance by taking wallpaper off her walls...Patient challenging herself.... walks six steps without support... Ambulates 100 feet with slight loss of balance twice.... 300 feet with standard cane.'"

"And all this was just prior to January 2007?"

"Yes."

The surrogate defense counsel on tape tries, as expected, to show that Valerie's current, post-suitcase, condition is largely the same as it was at the time of the suitcase accident. He suggests that one can't measure Valerie's pre-accident progress by looking at what kinds of canes she's using. Dr. Grill insists that you can indeed.

Roy's voice returns to redirect examination.

"What I want to make clear to the jury, Dr. Grill, is that you've been talking about courses of treatment. You had only *one* course of treatment that was after the suitcase incident, and your testimony has been that Valerie never got back after that course of treatment to where she had been before. Is that right?"

In real-time, Mr. Demerit starts to rise from his seat to object to the form of the question, but drops back down, recalling that he cannot challenge a video that his assistant had approved.

"She had not gotten back to the level prior to the suitcase accident."

At the close of the session, Demerit once again appears at Roy's desk.

"$750,000."

***

"Take it."

To Julie, a bird in the hand... "This is triple what they originally offered."

Sam chuckles easily. "What they originally offered was an insult—and believe me, they meant it as such... They never took this case seriously. Seriously, don't worry. They haven't even started to bargain... And I haven't even presented *my* experts: the numbers, dollars, and cents."

Later than night, on Sam's advice, Valerie and John again reject the defense's offer.

***

The next courtroom sessions are so dry that several of the court-as-entertainment spectators leave.

The topic is money and how damages in this case would be calculated.

Sam calls Cornelius Gorman, Ph.D. and partner in the life-care planning firm of Gorman & Gorman Inc. to testify.

Dr. Gorman's testimony summarizes a 50-page analysis of what it would probably cost to adequately care for Valerie throughout her life. It's a staggering amount.

That testimony is then put into perspective by Zoe Meeks, a Louisiana accountant, an expert in injury suits. She projects values, based on Federal statistics, life expectancies, interest rates, discount rates, etc., of both Valerie's income losses and future medical costs projected over her expected lifetime in 24 pages of detailed, explicit line items. It comes to $6,924,435.

***

Roy and Sam know they need to finish big. They meet with Valerie in her room.

"You're up tomorrow," Roy says. "How do you feel?"

She says, "Fine," but one look at her says otherwise. Dark circles outline her eyes, the result of not sleeping. Her hands quiver, not so much from spasticity this time, as from nerves. She looks sunken and worn. Not that Roy looks much better. He's been up most nights rehearsing, reviewing, anticipating.

"It's hard to read the jury," Sam says. "But I think they're coming around to our side. There couldn't be a better time for you—and John—to close the deal… Look, I'm going

221

to work on my closing arguments and leave you with Roy; he'll prep you so that you could do this in your sleep."

"What sleep?" Valerie says.

Sam smiles and departs.

"Okay, I know this is tough. You're nervous—everybody who ever testified is—that's normal. Thing to remember is that you're right, you're honest, there's nothing can change that."

Roy first goes over the basics: answer the defense's questions as briefly as possible. Yes or no would be best. Do not argue with the lawyer. Do not look at the jury. Be calm.

He prepares her for the possibility that the defense will come at her hard—that the lawyer will be nasty, insulting, and that she should not be rattled by that and should not retaliate. They go over probable defense questions. They go over Roy's questions.

Roy goes over the same ground with John. "You'll follow Valerie," he says. "They will try to discount your testimony—after all, you're Valerie's husband, you're biased, and you stand to gain from this… Here's how you deal with that…"

***

When Valerie wakens the next morning, John helps her to the bathroom where she vomits. Her hands tremble. Her head spins. John holds her. She takes a deep breath.

"I'll call Roy, have him get a postponement or something," John says.

"No. No, I'll be okay," Valerie says. "Let's get me washed and dressed."

When they arrive in court, Valerie's whole body shakes. She sees faces turn toward her and, to her, all of them appear mean and accusative. One face, that of The Federation's razor-faced VP is, in fact, harsh. She glares at Valerie with contempt as John brings her into the courtroom,

222

and continues her knife-eyed look when Valerie is called to the witness stand.

When John wheels Valerie to the stand, Valerie assembles her two, arm-crutches, rises and looks at the steps that loom between her and the witness chair. Each step is at least one foot high—huge to her eyes—and present a dicey prospect. John helps her navigate unsteadily up each one. As he does, Valerie hears The Federation VP snort an expression of mock-incredulity: "*Really?*"

Roy greets Valerie with deference and slowly elicits from her an account of the accident, her progress up until that point, and the diminishment of her abilities immediately thereafter.

As he nears the end of his list of questions, he pauses to look closely at his witness. He ponders whether or not he should ask for a recess before turning her over to the opposition, but they're so close. Here, he makes a mistake and decides to let it continue.

"Your witness," he says to Demerit.

The defense attorney smiles as he approaches Valerie, as if he can see right through her and, in fact, he can see that she fidgets and that her features look gaunt and fragile. She's weak and he can make use of that.

"Ms. Daniell, you must be facing some daunting medical bills, is that correct?"

"Yes."

"And with you being unemployed and without an income, would you say you are under some financial pressure?"

"Objection."

"Overruled."

"You may answer."

"Yes."

"So is it true that a big award from a company like the Federation of State Medical Boards, such an award would go a long way toward easing your financial difficulties?"

Valerie looks at Roy. He gives her a slight nod of support.

"Yes?"

"Is that a yes or a question?"

"A 'yes.'"

"So, Ms. Daniell, won't you admit that this whole lawsuit is just a scam that you, your husband, and high school cohort, Mr. Payne over there, concocted to defraud my client of funds in order to—"

"Objection."

"I withdraw the question."

But, of course, the damage is done—not so much to the jury's beliefs, but to Valerie. She sits, paralyzed anew by the vicious nature of the question. She's never been accused of anything wrong before, much less…fraud.

Demerit resumes.

"Now do you remember a Mr. Greg Sconce sitting near you on the American Airlines flight in '07?"

It takes some time before Valerie responds.

"Yes."

"Do you recall what he wore that day?"

"No."

"Could you describe him for us?"

"Um…"

Valerie's mind goes blank. She looks out into the faces of the jurors, the attorneys, the few spectators, they all blend into one sea of color. Who? What? She tries to focus and the first thing she sees is that damned, sneering woman in the creased suit and bleached-blonde hair. A rip tide of terror surges up from her gut.

"Am I keeping you from something?" the attorney says disingenuously pleasant.

"Your honor…" Roy pleads.

Judge Kaplan leans toward Valerie and says, "Do you need some water?"

She looks at the judge and moves her head from side to side.

"Could you describe Mr. Sconce for us?" Demerit asks again, with some impatience in his voice.

"Um, no. I don't remember." Valerie says.

"Why didn't you get off the plane immediately, before it left the gate?"

"Um… I didn't want to stay in Dallas. I—"

"Didn't want to stay in Dallas. So, you didn't feel the need for immediate medical care?"

The cross-examination goes downhill from there. It is a disaster for Valerie. In an almost trance-like state, she agrees with every set-up the attorney presents. She hesitates and stammers and can't remember important facts throughout the questioning. By the end of it all, she is vaguely aware that she's ruined her own case and that's that.

Roy looks at Sam. "Call up John," he says. "Right now."

John helps Valerie from the stand, into her wheelchair and rolls her toward the exit. He leans close to her ear and whispers, "You did fine."

"We'd like to call John Carpenter," Roy announces.

John pauses, then takes his time getting Valerie situated. He looks at her tenderly. Then his expression morphs into one of serene pleasantness, something cheery and relaxed —as though what comes next is going to be fun.

Roy's questioning of John takes the jury through his love story with Valerie, his commitment to her, his selfless care for her, his first-hand observations of Valerie's recovery and, following the suitcase incident, her decline. They cover the fact that John has known Roy since high school. John is relaxed, articulate, disarming and, occasionally, funny.

Roy, preempting the defense, asks, "So you are in love with Valerie?"

"Since high school and every day since."

"And because of this great love, you'd do anything for her?"

John laughs. "No. There are times when I will absolutely *not* watch *Days of Our Lives* with her."

As intended, the spectators chuckle and the ugly scene of Valerie's earlier testimony fades a little.

"What I mean is, if the stakes were high—like this trial, where you both stand to gain financially—wouldn't you do *anything* if it meant helping Valerie."

Evenly, steadily, John says, "Becoming a fraud, or a liar, or a criminal, or someone else like that would *not* be a help to Valerie."

"Thank you," Roy says. "Nothing further."

Demerit, as expected tries to discredit John's testimony as being tainted—at best—by love and devotion and, at worst, by greed. John remains pleasant and even tempered throughout, often turning the tables on Demerit and complimenting him on his imagination.

"Isn't it more probable than not, that, given all these circumstances, you and she and Mr. Payne over there—your longtime buddy—figured you could take advantage of this minor incident and turn it into a big payday?" Demerit thrusts.

John smiles like a patient parent toward an ignorant child. "I suppose a crime writer could construct a scenario like the one you've invented—my compliments, by the way—but it's actually more probable that friends rally to each other's aid just out of simple goodness—as when one friend suffers a catastrophe like the one inflicted by your clients on my wife. Having friends is not a crime, sir, and I, for one, won't ever apologize for having mine."

***

The defense, having lost ground, brings forth its own expert medical witness to rebut Dr. Lanig's testimony: Dr.

Ramon Diaz-Arrastia, professor of neurology at the University of Texas Southwestern.

During direct testimony, the doctor talks of various cases he's read about that have been somewhat similar to Valerie's but without the same consequences and of cases in which recovered spinal cord injury patients have simply deteriorated due to aging.

Demerit asks, "In your experience do patients with spinal cord injuries recover and then, over time, deteriorate—without any new trauma?"

"I have seen, over the years in my practice, several patients like that. Folks who had a very severe spinal cord injury and had recovered to the point where they were walking, and then as they got older, in some cases, 10, 15, 20 years later, they started to decline again."

In the spectator rows at the back of the courtroom, John leans over to Valerie and whispers, "This has nothing to do with anything."

Valerie whispers back, "Just wait."

When the defense finishes its questioning, Roy rises and strolls toward the stand. He smiles and greets the doctor warmly and respectfully. After a few preliminary questions, he asks, "Doctor how would you describe the fields that you teach?

"Well, my clinical specialty is epilepsy. My research is in a number of areas, but my main focus is in traumatic brain injury."

"Does traumatic brain injury include the field of spinal cord injury?"

"Well, there's an overlap, but usually not. They are two separate fields."

"Have you done any research within the field of spinal cord injury?

"No."

"Do you have a clinical practice?"

"Yes. It is focused on epilepsy."

"Does epilepsy have anything to do with trauma to the spinal cord?"

"Well, no. It has to do with trauma to the brain."

"Have you testified as an expert in lawsuits before?"

"Yes. Two of them. Both for the defense."

"Were brain injuries involved?"

"Yes."

"In those cases, what were you an expert in?"

"Neurology and traumatic brain jury."

"Doctor, you testified that three to five percent of spinal cord injury patients develop progressive deterioration without any additional trauma, is that right?"

"That's right."

"So the other 95 to 97 percent don't develop that condition, correct?"

"That's what the literature seems to indicate."

"And the literature is where you get that three to five percent number?"

"Yes."

"Do you consider that number to be exceptional?"

"No. I would say the syndrome is rare but not exceptional."

"Any disagreements with Dr. Lanig's testimony other than the 'rare' versus 'exceptional' terms?"

"No."

"You have heard the testimony of Rita Mohsin here?"

"I read her deposition and those of the other witnesses who were on the plane."

"Did you assume, in preparing your report for the defense that the suitcase did, in fact, hit Valerie on the head?"

"I did."

"And did you assume that it hit her forcefully?"

"Yes."

"Would you say that the more forceful the impact was, the more likely it was the cause of her subsequent symptoms?"

"Obviously."

"You believe Valerie had a tethered spine at the time this suitcase hit her on the head?"

"Yes."

"Did you see that Dr. O'Connor noted in his first report of his examination of Valerie after the accident that she had a swelling on the side of her neck?"

"I did note that. But it may not have made it into my report."

"And that would be *objective* evidence of an injury to her neck?"

"That's right."

"Which would support Valerie's version of this accident?"

"It would be objective evidence that she had some injury. That's right."

"You agree that the suitcase being dropped on Valerie's head may be the cause of the deterioration she experienced in 2007?"

"It is possible."

"Now earlier you told us that your specialty was in brain trauma and epilepsy, correct?"

"Yes."

"So then, would it be fair to say that you're not really qualified to offer opinions on spinal cord injuries?"

The doctor pauses and looks around the courtroom before answering.

"Well…Yes…. I guess that's right."

"Thank you. No further questions."

***

That night, Roy paces the floor of his room. He has delivered his closing argument to the drapes and the walls over two dozen times—making an adjustment here or there as he hears the sounds of his own words and decides that one phrase should be emphasized over another.

He has pages of handwritten notes on a yellow pad—his constantly changing monologue. But there are parts of the script that remain blank—except for one general note: "Finish with how you <u>feel</u>." How *does* he feel? he wonders.

Unlike his other cases, this one is personal—not a good thing for a trial attorney. Roy witnessed Valerie's remarkable comeback himself—from as far back as the initial injury in Sedona. He knows the truth. He's not just representing a case; he's trying to achieve justice, to create something good. Never mind the money, the stakes are far higher for him. It's his last chance.

He hasn't told Valerie that hers is his last case. He's been offered a chance to return to the bench and has taken it. He desperately wants to win this one—and that's not good. He tries to control his emotions, and goes through the speech one more time.

***

The final day of the trial finds a few new faces in the spectator rows. Some suits from Federation's insurance company slide into an aisle behind the defense. The easily amused cowboy is back, along with several of the recreational spectators who, like those who fast-forward their dvds, are back to see how it all ends.

By trial protocol, the plaintiff's attorney makes the first closing argument—Sam takes that role, focusing on the money side of things—followed by the defense, followed by the plaintiff's rebuttal to close the show—that one will be Roy.

Sam strides toward the jury as if toward a group of old friends just arrived at his barbeque.

"Ladies and gentleman," he begins in his syrupy drawl. "One thing I need to impress upon you is something that's a little difficult for folks to appreciate. That is: why would the employer of a negligent person be liable for their employee's negligence? Doesn't seem right at first glance, does it? In fact, it's not always the case. There are many times when an employer is not liable for the actions of their employees— but this isn't one of those times. You see, under Texas law, there are special tests that decide when the employer is liable and when they are not."

Sam walks back to his table and pulls a thick book from one of the stacks there. He opens to a bookmarked page and peers in.

He tries not to think of how important this one point is to the whole trial. Even if his team proves Rita Mohsin negligent, proves that the accident caused Valerie's injury and the injury resulted in huge damages.... if The Federation is not found liable also, then the whole trial will amount to an academic exercise—since Rita Mohsin can't possibly pay what will be required.

He says, "One of the most important of these tests is whether or not the employee had—and I quote: 'undertaken a special mission at the employer's direction. *Or* is otherwise performing a service in furtherance of the employer's business —with the express or implied approval of the employer—so that the employee is directed in the employee's employment.'... That's from Newsom v. Ballinger Independent School District, 2007, by the way.

"Under the undisputed facts of this case, Ms. Mohsin was *not* commuting to or from any office of her employer. Rather, she was traveling on a mission *for* her employer, under the direction of a *vice president*..."

Here Sam looks up and smiles kindly at the harsh blonde sitting next to Demerit. She gives him a knife-eyed grin in return.

"...by a means selected *by* the company travel agency and entirely paid for *by* the employer, without any personal deviations whatsoever... Consequently, the Federation *is* vicariously liable for the damages caused by Ms. Mohsin during the January 2007 incident. That's just the law and the plain facts.

"Now the defendant would have you believe something that is not true. The real world effect of The Federation's argument is if a teacher, salesman or employee traveling by car to a different state for his job hurts someone while driving there, the employer can wash their hands of the employee and not stand behind the employee who was furthering the business of the employer. The employee would then solely and individually bear all responsibility and the employer would walk away and abandon the employee in his time of need… that's why we have these laws and tests. That's why you must uphold them." Sam pauses and lets all that sink in before moving over to the money side of things, reiterating the details of previous testimony.

After that he reviews the facts of the case, of the accident itself, that Dr. Lanig confirmed all their contentions, that Dr. Lanig is not just a regular doctor but a specialist in rehabilitation medicine and in spinal cord injuries, that the defense presented no evidence, called no physician who ever treated Valerie, presented only one doctor—and that one was not even expert in the relevant field. He goes over the lower standard of proof in civil cases, the preposterous claims of the defense, the details of Valerie's suffering, the jury's oath and their duty to uphold it.

Throughout, he keeps an eye on the jury, trying to read them, trying to deduce when he should wrap it up.

He concludes with, "Is there anything that The Federation has to say that is worth believing? Remember you are the judge of the facts. As the Judge instructed you, if you find that a witness is not telling the truth you can disregard everything that witness says. The facts are clear. You will make the right decision. Thank you."

Sam returns to his chair.

Demerit rises, buttons his suit-coat and smiles at the jury.

"Ladies and gentlemen. Over the course of the past several days you have heard the plaintiff try to convince you of something even more difficult than employer liability. They would have you believe that a fragile woman who suffered a catastrophic injury eleven years ago, leaving lasting damage to her neck and spine, somehow recovered to such a degree that she was mentioned in a book about beating the odds—that itself should suggest something highly improbable—and that, having made this unlikely recovery, she was then sent all the way back to nearly the level of her original injury by the passing-by of a carry-on bag from just a few feet away.

"Luckily—or unluckily I should say—for Ms. Daniell, you cannot be sure what, if any, her level of recovery was from the year 2000 injury. You cannot know for sure that the passing-by of the bag caused any damage that wasn't already present. There's no way you can know any of this. Certainly, the plaintiff hasn't proven it.

"I mean, which do you think is more likely: that a disabled person facing financial trouble finds a way to blame a big company for damages supposedly suffered long after her injury; or that their loose and unprovable chain of events is true?

"Now, we're all in sympathy with Ms. Daniell's plight. All of us wish that she had not been hurt in the year 2000. We all feel bad for her physical and financial struggles… But sympathy is no reason to unjustly compensate her from the pockets of those who have no responsibility for her situation.

"Luckily for Ms. Daniell, her husband's good friend from high school is a personal injury attorney—a fairly successful one too, I understand. He came here all the way from Louisiana for this opportunity. Lucky also is the fact that they all found a way to go after a fairly prosperous and successful company—The Federation of State Medical Boards —in a hoped-for big-payday lawsuit. Naturally, they are asking for many millions—why not? Shoot for the moon. This is their big opportunity... Their scam... Don't let them get away with it. Don't let them play the system. It's not fair. It's not right."

Demerit nods, as if agreeing with himself, turns, glances at Roy, smirks and sits down.

Roy waits a minute before rising. When he does, he wanders over to the witness stand, puts on foot up on the first step and stays there a moment. He makes a move like starting to stand on the step, but then eases back down as if he thought better of it, or that the effort might be more than he could manage.

He turns and looks at the jury. His face and his voice are dead serious, indignant.

"The defendants are insinuating and accusing Valerie of making up a claim, hiring a lawyer early, and losing her job on purpose. Every witness in this trial talked about how Valerie is an inspirational, determined, hard working person. John Vernon did his work for free. Beth Grill said Valerie was a personal inspiration. Dr. Lanig saw how hard Valerie worked and her determination to get as good as she could be. Valerie is not the type of person who likes to make up a claim or to lose her job.

"The insinuation and accusation by the defendant is an insult to Valerie personally. The Federation insinuates and implies that Valerie got a lawyer very quickly in order to file a suit in an unnecessary and unjustified manner. You saw Valerie and John. You heard what type of person Valerie is. It is an absolute slander to Valerie. It is an insult to Valerie. It is a double insult when Rita Mohsin refuses to allow American Airlines to give out the incident report. This means that Valerie had no idea what happened to her. As a result, Valerie had to force American Airlines to give her the report. Valerie had to make an official legal request, in the proper form to American Airlines before they would even give her the report of what happened and who were the witnesses and who was responsible. Then the Federation wants to turn that around and use that fact against Valerie to insinuate that she was making a false claim!"

Roy pauses to rein in the volume of his voice. More calmly, but just as intently, he shakes his head and says, "This is an insult to Valerie. This is an insult to Valerie's lawyers. It is an insult without any basis in fact and is absolutely false.

"As a result of all this Valerie not only has to come here to make her legal claim, but she has been forced to defend her good name in the process.

"It's been said in a sports analogy that the best defense is a good offense. The Federation, instead of defending itself, is being offensive to Valerie.

"The defendant is asking you—by insinuating that Valerie is making a false claim—is asking you to look *outside* the evidence presented in this courtroom. You have given your oath to look only at the evidence produced by these witnesses. The Federation is asking you, as a juror, to violate your oath..."

Valerie's attention splits between watching Roy and watching the jury. Often, during Roy's strides, his body will block her line of sight, obscuring the jury's reactions, if any, from her view. On the occasions when she does have a clear view, the juror's faces and body language betrays nothing.

Roy pauses. He looks down and seems suddenly lost in thought. Valerie, seeing this, has a moment of panic: has he frozen?

Roy looks up. His voice shifts into a soft register. He swallows hard. His eyes, watery, reflect the courtroom lights. He speaks now off the cuff, just from the heart, pausing intermittently to gather himself.

"I've known Valerie for more than 40 years," he says. "I think this week you've gotten to know her, too. She's a giving person... One who has devoted her life to helping others. In school she had a passion for dance... But she didn't just pursue it for her own enjoyment. She discovered that she could use it to help deaf kids relate to the world that they were otherwise so cut off from... She got a Masters in Counseling for the Deaf at Gallaudet and went on to master sign language so she could work with deaf children.

"So you can imagine how devastating it was when she fractured her neck in that freak accident in 2000... But you've heard how she fought to overcome that injury. Within a year she was back living independently in Denver, walking with a cane, working as a counselor. Constantly getting therapy, constantly striving to improve... Then she reconnected with John, they married, she moved to Boston. She was working there as the Director of Counseling at the Walden School for the Deaf. You've heard from her therapists, Beth Grill and John Vernon, about how hard she worked and how much she had improved. ..

"There's no real question about what happened on that plane. You heard the sworn testimony of two completely independent eyewitnesses. Rita McMunn who was standing right behind Rita Mohsin, and Greg Sconce who was seated looking directly at Rita from the other side. Rita Mohsin made a half-hearted effort to stow the suitcase and as a result, dropped it right on Valerie's head. She showed no remorse, no concern. She came here and lied to you, saying repeatedly that her suitcase just 'brushed Valerie's hair.' But the truth is that it was a heavy blow, making a sound that Rita McMunn can't forget. It sent an electric shock through Valerie's neck and into her hands. You heard how Dr. Bean noted that "zinger" and the bruising in his records the next morning. You heard how she lost her job at the Walden School the next week when her hands started clawing and she lost her facility with signing."

Roy winces—not with lawyerly theatrics, but due to the genuine pain he feels just reciting the litany of sorrow heaped upon his friend.

"Dr. Indira Lanig, one of the best spinal cord injury specialists in the country, came here and told you that before the accident her patient Valerie was doing well, and that this accident started a deterioration that continues to this day. How because of the accident, Valerie had to undergo an extremely painful de-tethering surgery to try to stem the loss of muscle control. She told you what Valerie will need for the rest of her life to try to overcome this injury to her spine. Dr. Gorman told you what it costs, and Zoe Meeks told you what that means in today's dollars.

"Valerie has lived her life independently, striving and making her own way. In 2007, Rita Mohsin knocked her down a hill that is just too steep for Valerie to climb on her own.

"If you could turn back the clock and keep Rita from dropping that suitcase on Valerie's head, I know you would. But all you can do is follow the Judge's instructions and provide her fair compensation for the damage that's been done.

"Four years ago, she put her fate in my hands. Today, it is in yours. Thank you."

Roy returns to his chair.

Roy's daughter, Julie, now sitting next to Valerie looks at her and sees tears streaming down her face.

She takes Valerie's hand. Valerie smiles and cries at the same time and says, "Win or lose... What he said... what you all have done... That means everything to me."

After the jury leaves the room, Valerie, Julie and John remain sitting. To their surprise, Roy hasn't taken a single step back toward his table. Instead, he paces up and down in front of the empty jury box. His head bends downward, his arms fold across his body. To Valerie, he appears deep in thought; perhaps she detects a frown. Perhaps he's thinking they will lose.

What she doesn't know is that Roy has a lot going on. There's the release, the moment when the game ends, the pressure retreats, the tide of stress pulls away leaving a void deeper than a sigh. This case is over, yes. But so are all of his cases. He knows he won't try another. He also juggles and tries to find a place for his personal emotional ties to Valerie, John and his deep hopes for their well-being and how all of that is linked to the verdict. He's also sorting out the satisfaction he feels about his daughter having been at his side, working with him on this one.

What Valerie doesn't see, since, at that moment, Roy's back is to her, is his smile—the savoring of an immeasurably satisfying rush of all those emotions budding into something really fine… *They're going to win.*

Roy's reverie is disturbed suddenly. It's Demerit.

"High-Low," he says.

Roy looks steadily at the man who moments ago called him a scam artist. But he lets it go. His instinct is now confirmed. His opponent knows what he knows. The only thing now is the numbers.

"What are you offering?"

"Six million, high; 500,000 low."

Sam ponders it for a minute. "No appeal, plus no discount for prior monies received."

"Okay."

"I'll see what my clients have to say… I'll get back to you."

The "high-low" proposal works like this: even if Valerie loses the case, she'll get $500,000 from the defendant. If, on the other hand, the jury awards her something more than $6-million, she'll only get $6-million. If she wins, and the jury awards her something in between, she'll get that. The additional incentive to the offer is that the other side will never appeal the case and that whatever she received from Mohsin's homeowner's policy will not be deducted from the award.

Roy, Sam, Valerie, John, and the staff sit in the courthouse vending machine room eating sandwiches from the deli around the corner, letting the battle and fatigue of the past five days slip from their shoulders. Valerie and John have accepted the High-Low offer. The low end won't cover anyone's time and expense—much less provide for Valerie's recovery. On the other hand, it's better than nothing and they want Roy's losses to be minimized. Now it's just a matter of waiting to hear what the jury has to say.

The door to the room opens and Lori joins them. She's just flown in from Shreveport to lend her support. She hugs Valerie and then sits down with the group. The room is quiet; each person immersed in their own thoughts.

It's just before the President's Day holiday. Roy figures the odds are that the jury will make a decision soon—if for no reason other than to get the hell out of there.

A court clerk arrives in the room. "The judge is calling everyone back," she says.

"A verdict?" Roy asks.

"No. I think the jury is requesting something."

Roy turns to John. "False alarm. They probably want some document or another." He gathers up his briefcase and puts his suit-coat back on. "Heh, you know there's an old courthouse joke about a trial that goes the plaintiff's way and they find out they've won when the jury asks for a calculator. I don't know if that's ever happened in real life, but this would be a good time for it."

John chuckles politely—too tense now for real levity.

The entourages of both sides file back into court and take their places. A bailiff transfers a note from the foreman to the judge who reads it, then folds it again.

Kaplan says, "The jury has requested a calculator."

Roy nearly chokes trying to stifle a hoot and holler. He turns around to look at John and Valerie. For the first time that week, his eyes gleam. He mouths the word, *Ex-cell-ent!* John laughs out loud.

The jury again retires and Valerie's group goes to the courthouse lobby to wait.

"You think we've won?" Valerie dares ask.

"Well, I'd say we've won *something*," Roy ventures.

They sit in the lobby for two hours and are about to leave for the day when the clerk finds them. "They've reached a verdict," she says.

Valerie's heart jumps. All that time, all the stress, all the work and hope…it all comes to this moment. She swallows hard as John wheels her back into court.

After everyone returns and sits, Judge Kaplan looks at the jury box and at the foreman in particular.

Kaplan says, "Has the jury reached a verdict?"

"Yes, your Honor."

Kaplan gives the bailiff a hand-signal to take the questionnaire from the foreman and deliver it to him.

The judge takes the form, unfolds it, and reads aloud:

"'Does the jury find Rita Mohsin negligent in the matter before the court?… The jury finds… Yes.

"'Does the jury find The Federation of State Medical Boards vicariously liable for the negligence of its employee, Rita Mohsin?"

Here, Valerie, John and even Roy hold their collective breath. If the jury doesn't find that Mohsin acted in the course and scope of her employment, then anything else will mean little.

Kaplan reads, "The jury finds… Yes.'"

Roy looks at Valerie and John, nods once and offers a small smile.

By contrast, the company's glaring VP leans forward and snarls something under her breath at her attorney. He motions for her to relax. She grudgingly sits back.

"'As to the matter of damages—if any—to be awarded the jury finds:

"'For Lost Wages and Earning Capacity... Zero.'"

Valerie's throat chokes her. She closes her eyes and tries to swallow. Her mind is struck—not by her own disappointment, or the loss of compensation—but by the thought of the financial hit to Sam and Roy: all their work and huge expenses for nothing. She wasted their time, wasted the time and money of her good friend. She knows she's to blame. Her terrible performance on the stand earlier is the reason. It's all her fault, which creates an unbearable, new reality. She should never have done this.

For the first time in several days, the company's VP grins broadly. She pats her attorney on the shoulder and then gives Valerie one of those smirky, catty-schoolgirl sneers of triumph.

The judge continues. "'For Past and Future Physical and Mental Pain and Suffering... Zero.

"'For Past Medical Expenses...Zero.

"'For Loss of Enjoyment of Life...Zero.

John takes Valerie's hand. She fights back tears. Roy turns around to look at her and makes a gesture as if to say, "No big deal. Don't worry about it," or something similarly reassuring.

"And, 'For Future Medical Expenses...'"

Kaplan removes his glasses and looks at Valerie with what seems a gaze of sympathy. Without putting his glasses back on, or referring to the document in his hands, Kaplan looks fixedly at Valerie as he says, "Three million...four hundred sixty-two thousand, two hundred twelve dollars." He raps his gavel. "Court adjourned."

What? She hears the words, but cannot be sure. Did he really say that? Did we win the case? She looks at John, who smiles wider than she's ever seen, and who then leans over and kisses her for a very long time. When he pulls away, she sees that his eyes glisten.

"Oh my God." Valerie exclaims. "It's true? It's over. We won?"

The Federation's VP storms out of the room, but Valerie doesn't notice, much less use the moment to return some of the hateful looks she's received.

Roy, Sam and Lori each come to Valerie. Each in turn hug her, then hug John.

That evening the group pops champagne in Roy's room. They've ordered *hors-d'oeuvres* from room service and now sit or mill around what had been a work table in the room.

"Here's another bonus," Roy says, glass in hand. "Because they went to that high-low deal, they have no right to appeal, and… they must give you a check within 30 days."

"Woo. Hoo." Valerie and John crow at the same time.

"Roy… I don't know what to say… You put your heart and soul into this. You risked so much for me. All of you did. I really don't know how to thank you. It's all so much. I still feel like I'm dreaming," Valerie says.

Roy smiles and shakes his head, a little awestruck himself. John comes up and puts an arm around Roy. He says nothing, but the gesture says it all.

Finally, Roy takes a breath and says, "I admit, I've never been more satisfied… So now you have both justice and some money. That's as it should be… But this trial, what I did, what you did…what of all of us did—that was the easy part… The hard part's coming up… The hard part's living. The hard part's going to be the long climb ahead."

Twenty-One — Limón

Limón technique:
   A modern dance technique developed by Jose
   Limón, based on "fall, recovery, and rebound."

Valerie's second climb back begins long before any court verdict. It's a litany of work, surgery, continual physical therapy, setbacks and steps forward that can be summarized as follows:

2008

Untethering surgery.
   As described in the trial, untethering is a difficult procedure to remove scar tissue wrapped around the spinal cord. The risk associated with the procedure is paralysis. Valerie is in the hospital for 16 days, enduring excruciating headaches.
   Recovery is complicated by a spinal fluid leak. The leak is located and stitched, leaving a nine-inch scar.
   Mobility improves slightly.

2011

Lumbar drain.
   Excess accumulation of spinal fluid, causing Valerie's hands to seize again. In the hospital for six days. Hand function improves.

<u>Knee braces</u>.

When Valerie tries walking in therapy, her knees hyperextend—a new malady. She's fitted with two knee braces that prevent her from sitting and require her to put them on every time she wants to walk. Over time her legs regain strength and the braces are discontinued.

<u>Shunt surgery.</u>

A drain system, not unlike Hilary's, is inserted to manage fluid build-up. She's in the hospital 11 days. This is followed later by corrective surgery to adjust the shunt tube that had moved and knotted.

2012

<u>Accidental fall</u>.

Valerie breaks four toes. Requires a scooter to get around. Physical therapy sessions lack some walking aspects as a result.

Joins PEAK (Performance, Exercise, Attitude and Knowledge) Program at Craig Hospital—a special rehabilitation program. There she meets Kaci Young, a dedicated physical therapist, with whom she will develop a deep friendship. Works out twice a week.

2013

<u>Contracts C Diff</u> (Clostridium difficilecolitis), an infection of the digestive tract. Six months required to arrest the infection.

<u>Twists ankle</u> on a rehab machine. Physical therapy delayed a month. Ankle problems persist.

<u>Second Lumbar drain</u>.

Excess accumulation of spinal fluid, causing Valerie's hands to seize again. In the hospital six more days. Hand function improves.

Corrective shunt surgery.
Cleans out out clogged shunt. In the hospital for five days.

2014

Shunt tube removal.
Device misaligned and pokes at Valerie's gall bladder. Shunt surgically removed.

Ankle brace prescribed.

2015

Reinsertion of shunt.
Excess accumulation of spinal fluid, causing Valerie's hands to seize up. It is hoped the shunt and subsequent drainage will improve hand function once more.

***

The really significant thing about Valerie's struggles is that, throughout them, she keeps an eye on opportunities to help others.

In 2011, Valerie arrives at Craig Hospital the night before surgery for the insertion of her first shunt. She is taken to her room and finds she will have a roommate, a woman of about 35, a mother of five.

That evening, while sitting in a chair playing Scrabble by the dim light of an iPad, Valerie jumps at the sound of a harsh voice.

"Turn out the damn light. I need it dark to sleep."

Valerie turns off the device.

When the evening nurses arrive to check on the patients, the roommate greets them with, "What the hell?. Go bother someone else."

The nurses leave and Valerie rises, gets in her wheelchair, and moves down the hall toward the nurses' station. She's nervous about the surgery and can't sleep anyway, so why not talk with the staff?

"My roommate seems a bit... testy," Valerie says to one of them.

"A testy bitch is what she is," one of them replies. "I shouldn't say that. Sorry."

"What happened to her?"

"You'd have to ask her."

"Obviously, she's angry."

After her surgery, Valerie lies flat for three successive days. On the second day, the curtain between her and her roommate parts and her roommate wheels herself in. Her arms and neck are plastered with tattoos.

"What's your problem?" the woman says.

"No problem," Valerie insists, reflexively on the defense with this one.

"No, I mean, what happened to you? Whadda ya in for?"

"A shunt."

Valerie gives the woman a brief summary of her whole story, after which the woman sits next to Valerie's bed and sighs.

"I'm sorry," she says. "I thought *I* had it bad."

The woman shares her story. She'd been sitting at her kitchen table, stood up and collapsed. She has some kind of spinal cord tumor. She begins to talk about her biker boyfriend, her kids, her second floor apartment that has no elevator, and finally, the anger she feels toward God for giving her the damn tumor.

"It's life changing, isn't it? And so unexpected," Valerie says, validating the woman's feelings. "It's okay to feel angry… I sure did."

"You're goddamn right."

"For me, I chose to express my anger to others—but not to take it out on them. I'd just tell people, frankly, how angry I was."

"Makes sense."

"So, how would you like to see your life five years from now?" Valerie asks. "What do you need to do to make sure your children are taken care of: their immediate needs handled?"

The woman ponders the question, but the point of it —as Valerie the psychotherapist intends—is to direct the woman's outlook forward to disconnect her, even momentarily, from her present anger.

Over several days, the two continue to talk, with Valerie doing most of the listening. Sometimes, the woman comes to Valerie; sometimes they converse through the curtains.

"What should I do?" the woman asks at one point.

"One thing is you should focus on whatever stage of recovery you're in. Adapt. Be ready to solve problems—you know, with transportation, wheelchairs, SSDI, whatever comes up."

***

A couple of years later, Valerie encounters the same woman at a Craig outpatient clinic.

The woman, in a wheelchair, says, "I've thought about you and wondered how you were doing." She smiles.

"I'm just fine," Valerie says. "You?"

"I'm fine too."

Twenty-Two — Freedom Dancing

"I loved dancing because, for me, it was freedom."

Valerie's words play in my head as my wife and I drive through tens of thousands of acres of free-range sage, taking a short-cut from Santa Fe to Denver to meet with John and Valerie Carpenter to discuss the book. As it happens, we'll be spending most of Independence Day weekend with them at their suburban home.

We roll down the windows and let the cool dawn air of the high plains sweep through the car and bring with it the perfume of the sage brush which is almost intoxicating. The low, morning sun paints long shadows behind the foothills and longer shadows behind one of the 14,000-foot peaks coming into view. Ours is the only vehicle on the road this early in the morning. Since the book occupies my thoughts, I scan both exterior and interior landscapes for metaphors.

The obvious one, of course, is the fact that this visit coincides with the Fourth of July and thus there are natural tie-ins to concepts of independence and Valerie's life-long desire for freedom and her fights to regain it. I have the sense that freedom is a moving target, a goal no one fully achieves, but a good one nonetheless.

The mountains, of course, present another symbol. Before the accident, Valerie hiked several of Colorado's 53, 14,000-foot-plus peaks. Since then her mountains have taken on a different look.

So far, we have about ten chapters done and a good idea about the tale's direction, but it's high time for a visit, as I haven't seen Valerie for five years, not since our Langley High School class reunion in 2010.

I recall seeing her then—the first time since graduation 40 years earlier. I'd heard nothing about her in the intervening years. My first sight of her at the reunion found her seated in a chair near the front door of the old, weathered Great Falls Grange building which served as the evening's dance hall. Her life-long friend Lori Fuller sat next to her as they watched John Carpenter's old band, *The Incredible Fog*, reunited for the evening, play rock tunes to which their classmates danced as in the old days. A pair of crutches leaned alongside her. An ankle boot anchored one foot.

I asked Valerie what had happened and heard a quick summary of her tale and of a pending trial regarding the suitcase incident. By the time she finished, I told her I thought her tale worthy of a book and that she should write one. Naturally, telling someone *else* they should write a book requires no great effort on one's own part.

Nearly five more years passed before I received an email from Valerie saying that she'd written her book and would I, being a writer, like to read it and comment. Of course I would. But the manuscript's arrival let me down. The whole thing amounted to a 28-page summary. *Twenty-eight pages?. No, no, no. Come on, Valerie. This will never do. Your story deserves far more. This is an insult to yourself.*

Imagine getting indignant when someone gives short shrift to *their* life story, not yours. We corresponded after that until Valerie offered to hire me to do the job. I cautioned her against it, if she wanted the fortune and glory of a best-seller, or a tv movie, or even simply getting a traditional publisher. I told her of the astronomical odds against any of those things happening—even if you had the best story ever.

"Remember," I said, "Even *Moby Dick* didn't catch on until long after Melville was dead—and even so, he had to self-publish it. Do you really want to go through all the work and expense of something like this? What you need to ask yourself is, 'What do I really want out of this?'"

Without hesitation she said that if the book could help even one other person in a similar situation, then that's what she wanted and it would be worth it. I told her I believed we could achieve that much, and so we started.

Now months into the project, I know what the story is about and it's not what I first thought. Initially, it seemed like a saga of someone overcoming tragedy, salvaging her life with the help of an innate positive outlook, guts, true love and loyal friends. True enough, those factors come into play, but now I see it more as a circle. A journey in which the hero leaves and returns to where they began. Valerie has the heart of a true caregiver. Her battle, the reason she fights for her independence, is so that she can help people once again—the way she did before the accident. I should have realized that from the beginning. Even her highly solicitous preparations for our arrival evidenced her other-directedness: "Are there any foods you don't like?" "Allergic to anything?" "What do you like to drink?" "Do you like coffee, or tea?" "When do you like to rise?" "I have a present for Karla." (I take her at her word and relate that I don't consume carbohydrates—not even in beer, but will drink straight spirits).

Anyway, now I want to see how the Carpenters live today, ergo the long and beautiful drive through Colorado to their home.

The approach to Littleton makes me think of Valerie's McLean, Virginia back in the 1960s. Suburban tracts give way to large, open fields of high, wild grasses, bordered by leafy deciduous trees of various types. If I could ignore the mountain range and the absence of high humidity, I could imagine myself as a boy in the Old Dominion once again.

A few turns more and we glide onto a heavily-shaded avenue canopied by ancient cottonwoods, elms and maples. The Carpenters' house comes up on our right—a split-level, ranch-style home of handsomely stacked, grey stonework sitting on at least a half-acre of land.

Valerie, in a motorized scooter, and John greet us at the front door. Turns out that the scooter has more to do with a recurrent ankle ailment than with her neck issues and that, ordinarily, she can navigate with canes or crutches. Either way, the entry level of their home—where most of the living is done—has no drops or stairs to impede her movements.

Greetings exchanged, we take a quick tour. The living room is just to the right of the entrance and the first thing you see is a Steinway grand piano—John's instrument. I make a mental note to ask him later if he will play something for us. Most of the decor features Valerie's substantial and tasteful collection of antiques.

The home takes advantage of skylights and so, is well-lighted and open-feeling all day. The master bedroom features a custom, lowered bed frame (I remember that John Carpenter actually is a carpenter in his spare time) more conducive to Valerie's movements. The bathroom, toilet and shower, are also explicitly designed to accommodate Valerie's requirements: you can roll a wheelchair into the shower for example.

Another room nearby is dedicated to in-home physical therapy. It holds a mat table, a recumbent bicycle, exercise balls, hand weights, weighted balls, step platforms, resistance bands, wall support bars and a good source of music. Twice a week, Valerie's physical therapist for the past three years, Kaci Young, comes over to see Valerie through her regimen. I make a note to ask if we can see a session.

We will stay downstairs, a quiet, cool level dedicated to guests. It has its own pool table.

With the tour complete, we relax out back, beneath a covered patio that opens onto a shaded backyard lawn, throughout which stand bird-feeders, bird-houses, butterfly houses, all ringed by maple, ash, pine, and cottonwood trees of substantial girth. Birdsongs fill the air. We catch up and discuss a few book-related topics, one of which is the state of HP-184.

Months ago, after hearing the disheartening story of how Sanofi-Aventis pulled its effective drug from Valerie and people like her, I suggested a radical plan, based on my old philosophy that if the game is rigged against you, cheat. I did some scouting around. Drugs are usually patented before clinic trials which would mean that the formula for HP-184 should be available via the Patent Office. Sure enough it is. So I asked Valerie and John—in purely theoretic terms—if they knew a gifted chemist who, given the formula, could make it for them. I figured that the main reason for patents is to prevent one from making and then *selling* the product. Since, in this scenario, they wouldn't be selling it, then perhaps there wouldn't be any infringement problem.

A crazy idea, perhaps, but you never know. I ask if they'd investigated it any further. John surprises me by saying that, in fact, they had.

"We actually do know someone who works for a compounding pharmaceutical company and talked to him about this," John says. "The problem is that there is one more aspect to it, not included in the patent. Evidently, the key is how the drug is metabolized—a process that makes the body *use* the drug rather than just excrete it. That's the secret. Figuring that out would be prohibitively expensive."

I present Valerie with a gift: a fifth of Casamigos Anejo tequila—the best stuff I've ever tried; it tastes more like caramel-vanilla candy than alcohol.

"You might not want to mix this with anything," I advise. "It's sipping tequila. Let me know what you think."

There's a reason for this particular gift. Though Valerie smiles and appears completely at ease, prickly, electric pain shoots through her skin most of the time to varying degrees. It's the nerve pain that comes with spinal cord injuries. She describes it as feeling that her nerves lie on the outside of her skin—a sensation akin to someone pouring gasoline on her and lighting a match, a constant burning—for the past 15 years. One night, when the pain robbed her of sleep, she mixed some tequila with orange juice. The skin pain stopped for a while. One shot of it. No other alcohol works.

Similarly, another ongoing affliction suffered by many patients of spinal cord injuries is a spastic leg syndrome that occurs when lying down at night. One's leg muscles suddenly and violently contract without warning. Those who experience the syndrome might wake to find they have kicked their spouse right out of bed. Some barely sleep at all.

Sedatives are most often prescribed for the problem, but of course, the drugs come with their own problems and, in Valerie's case, have little effect.

"What you have to know about Valerie," John says, "is she's your quintessential straight arrow. She never partied in high school; she's never done drugs; never even smoked a cigarette. She's always frowned on that stuff. I'd heard that marijuana helped this guy who had the same spasming problem, so—very cautiously—I told Valerie about it and asked her to consider it. The problem got so bad that she finally consented.

She got a prescription for medical marijuana. John bought some special cookies. Valerie tried one before bedtime. Problem instantly solved.

But Valerie, not wanting to be thought of as a "pot-head," takes great pains to point out that she *only* takes the small-dose cookie at bedtime and *only* to control the night spasms. I don't doubt it for a second.

Besides being a 24/7 caregiver, maestro pianist, composer, carpenter (he also did the cabinets in the house), and, according to himself, an average golfer, John is an excellent chef. He has steaks, asparagus, and some kind of sweet-potato concoction going in the kitchen.

Valerie and I sit in the living room, going over old photographs and documents from her past, trying to sort out what might be useful for this story and what is simply interesting from our shared experiences as kids. At one point, she picks up a small, turquoise necklace from the cluster of articles.

"That's pretty," I say.

"I got this in Sedona, the day before the accident. My ex-boyfriend—the one who dumped me afterwards—he helped me pick it out... I've never worn it."

Of the two of us, Valerie is the psychotherapist and yet I suppose, like great hairstylists who can't cut their own hair, Valerie doesn't seem to be able to see what seems obvious to me—she has given this thing power, and thus has given the unworthy boyfriend an unearned power too. It is irrational, of course, but still powerful. I reason, then and there, that an irrational illness might be fixed with an irrational cure.

I hold out my hand. "May I hold it?" I ask. She drops the necklace onto my palm. I close my palm around it, then close my other hand around the first.

"Where is the necklace now?" I say in the manner of one doing a common disappearing magic bit.

"In your hand," Valerie points.

"Are you sure?"

"Yes."

"It is completely surrounded by *my* hands. Correct?"

"Yes."

I blow into my fists, then speak in the best Wizard of Oz-like voice I can muster.

"Using my *mana* (a Hawaiian term for spiritual power) I now extinguish all the evil mojo in this thing and imbue it with its own beauty. It is now a newly created thing."

I open my hands, smile, and hand the necklace back to Valerie. She chuckles and puts it away.

John presents a fine steak dinner. We drink some Belle Glos pinot noir. The conversation rambles over a variety of topics—not book-related necessarily, just the type of things couples talk about at dinner—all of our various terrible ex-spouses, how reckless and stupid we were in our youth, the era when we were all immortal. I ask Valerie how her dexterity is, can she still sign?

She says her signing is no longer at its best, but that she can still communicate. "My deaf friends say I speak with a lisp now," she laughs.

We talk about our "bucket lists." Valerie's is exact. She aims to:

—Go to future Langley High School reunions.
—Have a fun car to drive; a Mini Cooper preferably.
—Visit old friends around the country.
—Visit the set of *Days Of Our Lives.* Meet the actors she's watched since childhood.
—See the look on John's face when he sees the Northern Lights for the first time.
—See the sunrise on the red rocks of Sedona that she never got to see that awful morning.
—Walk without a cane.
—Put her toes in the sand and ocean.

"So people will probably want to know what enabled you to handle everything that's happened. What would you say to them?" I ask.

Valerie thinks for a time, takes a breath and shrugs.

"Well, the accident was the moment where my life changed of course. It was the death of something old making way for something new. I discovered that life is better with a positive attitude. Material objects—a nice house, what kind of car you drive, what kind of clothes you wear—at the end of the day those things don't matter as long as you have family, friends and love. Never underestimate the power of the mind and the power of attitude. Your outlook is the difference between living and just existing. No matter how bad life may seem at the time, it *can* get better."

"That's what you learned, but what got you to that point?"

"I guess I needed courage or… what would you call it? Tenacity? And persistent effort to push myself through rehabilitation and to find solutions to the day to day problems of living with a disability."

"What if you just don't have those things? What if you just weren't born with a positive attitude?"

"It's there. You have it. It's just up to you to find it."

She pauses, evidently trying to recall more.

"Back at Baylor, I prayed to God every day to help me through this dreadful episode. I wanted to prove everyone wrong. I begged, bartered, pleaded and promised that if I could get better I would help others who needed encouragement to overcome their disabilities. I had three college degrees and experience as a counselor and deaf interpreter and I swore I'd use those skills again, and thus prove there was life after a catastrophic injury. I swore that if I could get the use of my hands back, I'd once again help deaf people cope with their private, silent world.

"I had an epiphany one day. It was like some kind of exhilarating sensation sweeping over me. I just had an overwhelming urgency to prove everyone wrong. I said to myself that I was going to walk again. I even had a dream where I was walking up the stairs of my townhouse with a cane. It was so vivid and real. I kept that vision in my mind everyday.

"The key was attitude. It was everything. A negative attitude makes life depressing. Fighting through depression wears you down. Disabled people have to figure out how to keep living with the death of their old selves, and how to create new selves. I like this quote: 'When something bad happens you have three choices. You can let it define you, let it destroy you, or you can let it strengthen you.'"

On the morning of the Fourth of July, I receive a phone call from an old friend who also lives in Denver. We'd made tentative plans to meet the following day, but he'd like to know if my wife and I can join him this afternoon for a few hours for a casual party. John and Valerie have already said they have no special plans for the Fourth and, since it's okay with our hosts, we accept.

Before we go to the celebration, a tall, pretty, athletic-looking woman of around 30, with long blonde hair, Kaci Young, Valerie's physical therapist, arrives. She wears a neon-pink tank top and yoga tights. She and Valerie hug at the door then go to the exercise room.

"Kaci puts me through the paces," Valerie grins. "She doesn't let me get away with anything."

"Ha. I don't have to do that much. Valerie is the one always wanting to do more, do something harder."

"Oh, I don't know," says John. "Kaci is like Valerie's Marine Corps drill instructor."

Kaci, a former volleyball player, smiles demurely. "I provide enthusiastic encouragement," she clarifies.

They begin the process. Today it starts with the mat table. Valerie lies on her back while Kaci, sitting alongside, pushes a leg back toward Valerie's midsection in a stretching move. After that, Kaci will kneel on the table at Valerie's feet and provide resistance as Valerie does core-crunching work. After that, Valerie sits on the edge of the table and does partial stand-ups to a near squat before lowering herself again.

"We found that Valerie is perfectly able to stand upright, but that if she extends her arms in front of her, or to the sides, it throws off her balance. It's like the weight wants to pull her toward it. So we practice that," Kaci says. "I'm right there to steady her if needed."

Valerie, sore ankle and all, takes on a pair of crutches and walks around the room, out the door, down the hall and back, with Kaci in tow.

The two of them have worked together for over three years and one can see that they've developed a bond. Valerie takes a rest and sits on the mat table again; Kaci sits beside her.

"We're not just client and therapist," Kaci volunteers. "We're very close. Valerie is someone I really like."

"We're like family. We share confidences." Valerie agrees.

"What in particular do you like about Valerie?" I ask.

Actually, the question seems ordinary and I expect nothing special to come of it other than a friendly testimonial, which is why her response or, more accurately, her delivery knocks me out.

"She's my hero," Kaci says. Immediately her eyes fill with tears, her voice quavers and she sobs throughout the rest of her statement. "She goes through so much... and yet she has such a positive outlook. She's affected me so much..."

There's a momentary pause, as all of us, including Kaci, seem stunned by the outpouring of emotion. After a few moments, I ask: "Do you see yourself in Valerie? You're both caregivers; both athletes, as well as women."

Kaci nods, wipes her face and eyes, then laughs, embarrassed. "I don't know what's come over me... I've never done that."

Valerie moves closer and hugs her.

Another unexpected consequence of the book process: it has provided Kaci with an opportunity to tell Valerie how much she loves her.

Later that afternoon, we drive to nearby Arvada to attend my friend's festivities, enjoy some barbecue and catch up on conversation. My friend is a recently retired orthopedic surgeon.

At one point, the topic of conversation moves to Alzheimer's disease and from there to caregiving (his brother recently had to give up being the sole caregiver for their 90-

259

year-old mother). My friend mentions a study he'd recently read in the *Journal of the American Medical Association*. It looked into the mortality rate of relatives who became the sole caregivers for their elderly kin. Astonishingly, it found that 68 percent of the *caregivers* died before the elderly person. I filed that fact away for another time, then forgot about it.

We return to the Carpenters' house just after sundown to discover that Valerie has already gone to bed. Evidently, just after we'd left, she had driven her scooter around a corner, unaware that her toes protruded just slightly outside the frame of the thing, and crashed one of her toes into the wall, perhaps breaking the toe.

I find John sitting outside, under the roof of the darkened patio, with a couple of beer bottles near him. Clouds shroud the sky overhead. Fireworks and summer lightning compete to make the clouds pop erratically with light. I sit down and listen as John recounts the accident, which evidently included some spilled blood. He recites the events in a matter of fact voice. Then, in the middle of a sentence, both his tone and topic transform abruptly. His tone becomes oddly petulant; his topic, suddenly unrelated to its predecessor.

"What you don't understand," he exclaims, "is that we can't be spontaneous. We can't just change plans and do this or that. Our whole life is carefully planned out to the last detail."

"Okay…" I wait.

"What I'm saying is that none of those books report —not one of those books on people with spinal cord injuries —not one of them ever talk about the huge issue of controlling one's bowels. Not one. It's not just about trying to walk. It's not just walking that's affected. It's all your organs. How would you like trying to go out for dinner, or travel someplace and not know what might happen? We have to plan our weeks—what days will be open and what ones we'll have to stay in to take care of business. Nobody talks about that. Maybe it's too indelicate. But if we're going to continue with this book, then I think that has to be in there—so people who are going through it know that they're not alone. You haven't done that so far."

At first, I think John's sudden diatribe springs from deep anxiety over Valerie's toe accident that night, but its content doesn't match. It certainly isn't about the book neglecting anything: those excretory issues had already been mentioned in the manuscript thus far.

Was he upset, after all, that we visited the other friends for a few hours? Was he upset that we had not been there to help him mend Valerie's toe? I sit back and listen.

"We maintain this facade of normalcy for people," John complains. "We hide the way things really are—how difficult everything is, how much planning and accommodation goes into every little thing. All to make other people think we've adjusted and now things are all right. It's never all right. Listen. Finding Valerie is the best thing that's ever happened to me—don't get me wrong. I can handle anything; I think the time I spent with Hilary enabled me to handle anything. Anyway, I'm just trying to tell you the way things really are. I keep watch every second of every day. Even when things are humming along smoothly, I'm trying to anticipate what bad thing could happen next, so I can prevent it."

"You must be under constant stress," I say.

"Got that right. But that's what I do, that's what I signed up for. I am finally the man I'm supposed to be, rather than the selfish creep I'd been before."

I look at the bottles. It's the Fourth of July and a man with things on his mind is working through them. I'm glad his emotional door has opened.

"Have you been sitting here, dwelling on this all evening?"

John calms down a bit.

"Yes."

After a few moments, he resumes at a more relaxed pace.

"You see, Valerie wants things to be normal, so she pretends; she acts like things are normal. She doesn't tell you everything."

"Maybe she needs that. They say sometimes if you act happy long enough, you'll think you're happy. Personally, I think denial can be a good thing—in many situations."

"But if this book is going to be true—"

"It *is* true. But maybe it doesn't need to be comprehensive. Maybe there's a reason the other books don't go into some of those things... What if people—especially those with this injury—what if what they really need is hope? I figure they probably already know how much things suck. Maybe they need to focus on the good that's possible in order to achieve it."

John sighs. "Maybe so."

"May I have a beer?" I ask.

A shocked look comes to John's face. "I thought you didn't drink beer."

"Sometimes you have to break your own rules."

In the morning, John and I are the first up and the first to fill our coffee mugs.

"I want to apologize for last night," John says. "I was upset from the crisis with Valerie's toe."

"No need for that. I think you raised some valid points, some good things to think about."

We move from the kitchen to a sitting room. In a few moments, we're joined by the ladies.

"What did I miss last night?" Valerie asks.

"We had a good pow-wow. It's all good," I say.

"Okay... well, let me ask you this: looking ahead, what are the steps toward publishing this?"

I go over the options and sequences. On one hand, they can shoot for the stars, try to get a big publisher and see how that goes. One downside to that is it takes a great deal of time and patience, with no certainty of success. Another downside is the fearsome logistics of having to travel on a book tour—not to mention the loss of privacy and the utter destruction of the Facade of Normalcy.

On the other hand, they could go via print-on-demand. The upside of that is its immediacy, the control, the negligible publishing cost. A book could be produced and placed into the hands of SCI patients, or their families, virtually overnight. The downside is trying to market the book themselves.

We've spoken of these things before, but today they seem to present a real quandary.

"Going through all this just for the sake of a few people seems like a really expensive thing with little return," John suggests.

"You're right about that," I say, "*If* you're talking about money—but like I said from the start, making money is highly unlikely. But Valerie told me if the book could help just one person with an injury like hers have faith that there is life afterwards, that they can still have love in their life, then it would be worth it. Is that still the way you feel, Valerie?"

She nods emphatically yes.

I continue. "Let me suggest that doing this book—any book for that matter—can achieve a lot more; things you wouldn't think of at first. For example, just putting your life down on paper can add order and meaning to what might have been chaos and confusion.

"Not only that, but a book can be an exorcism—all the bad, all the evil, all the harsh times, they are literally and figuratively *bound* within the confines of a book." I pick up a random book lying nearby, open it, then slap its covers shut between my hands in a demonstration. "You own them now. You control them. You make them your prisoners right here

263

and now. You can open this book or close it, bring it out or confine it to a shelf. You can turn the page, shut the book, close the chapter, and move on." I open the book and slap it shut again.

John's eyes widen like those of a boy seeing the ocean for the first time. And now, just now, I understand what the previous night's conversation had really been about. It had been about pain and fear. John feared the *process* of putting the book together. Of being interviewed, of remembering too vividly. He feared having to relive all the past pain of his life. He feared going through it all again when he'd tried so hard to push it away, push it deep into some dark cave where he'd never have to see it. I think it may have been the mention of exorcism, or perhaps it had to do with the idea of creating a cage from a book, but we'd somehow found a safe harbor in which to evade those fears. You can almost see the burdens rise from him like evaporating mists.

Now enthusiasm returns. "However we go—shoot for the stars, or pass it around by hand—this book can help some people," Valerie declares.

I agree. "In various ways, I should think—besides being a comfort or an inspiration. I mean, theoretically, maybe, it could embarrass the suits at Sanofi-Aventis so they might finally make their drug available, do some good."

"I'd be happy if it would just open some doors at Craig Hospital," Valerie says. "Did you know that, before the suitcase thing, we went to Craig and said, 'Hey look, I'm a psychotherapist. I know sign language. I've *been* through spinal injury. So many of your patients could use my counseling abilities.' But we never had any response."

"So maybe this book could open that door," John says.

"Right. You never know what might come of this whole thing," I say.

I look over at Valerie and notice that she's wearing her now-redeemed turquoise necklace. Independence Day.

The morning of our departure, as I pack in the downstairs guest room, the rich sounds of the Steinway drift down from the living room above. I put my bag aside and climb the stairs to find John playing for the first time during our visit. I move silently to a chair to one side of his bench. His eyes are closed. His head and body bob and sway to the passion of the music.

I know what I'm hearing: John's sonata depicting the life of his daughter Hilary, composed in her memory. Again, music is so hard to describe in words, but trust me,* this rich tribute is so full of passion and compassion that you feel it as much as hear it. Its prevailing mood is tenderness and throughout you feel someone's deep, soul-penetrating love, their unbearable loss and their gratitude for a life. I realize what it is to "go slack-jawed." I become vaguely aware that my mouth is wide-open; eyes seeing only a blur through their own moisture.

When the last note vibrates away, I can only rise, step over to John, pat him once on the shoulder and walk into the next room.

I hear him breathe in and say, "That felt really good."

I shake my head and can only utter, "My, my."

* [You can hear the music at http://tinyurl.com/powsn2b]

The four of us cluster in the foyer, preparing our goodbyes. Valerie starts to push up out of her scooter, but I ask her not to; tell her to let me just bend down for a hug.

"No. I want to," she insists, and stands up and puts her arms around me. I appreciate both the emotion and the athleticism behind that simple move. If we sway in that embrace, let's call it a dance.

"Well, I guess that's that," I say. "I figure we'll have another six months or more to go on this."

"I'm excited," says Valerie. "We're going to help some folks again. This is going to have a happy ending."

"Yes," I say. "I think it will inspire a fair number of people who just might need it. As for endings… I don't think this thing has an ending. We're all just works in progress, eh?"

Valerie just smiles.

We pull out of the Carpenters' neighborhood and head due west, aiming at the Rockies. When we reach our main route through the mountains, I downshift, anticipating the long climb ahead.

Notes and thanks from Valerie

What used to be depression, is now resolve. My life is, what it is, and I accept it. Still, I will never give up hope for stem cell or some kind of cure for spinal cord injuries. I am always open to being a guinea pig for research, clinical drug trials, or anything that could advance science for the future.

I stay positive. I keep moving forward because to stop or give up is just not an option. I often think of what Gramma would say to me now. I think she would say, "Vaddie, don't you ever give up. Live your life the best you can. I am with you all the time." And she is....not only in her quilts, antiques, recipes and crocheted lace, but in her pioneer spirit that's with me always.

In times of crisis the old cliché that you find out who your true friends are is right on. Friends and acquaintances came through for me with some remarkable acts and constant moral support. During my struggles, I received so many flowers, plants, phone calls, visits, gifts, cards, hugs and words of encouragement from my friends... I honestly could not have gotten through it without them and their love and support. One can never underestimate the power of friendship and love when going through a crisis and catastrophic injury. So I'd like to thank, in no particular order:

Annie Hansborough Durloo, my fellow dancer, who brought me a boom box, music, haircut, movies, ice cream, food, shopping excursion and new clothes; Cheryl Blehm-

Poskus, for the crafts; Jill and Tim Wayne, who kept my private practice office going for me, and sold my house, taking no commission; Beth Grill for her constant encouragement and positive direction in many PT sessions; Jill Boice, for sending me books and a wind up toy with two yellow tennis shoes that walked; Ali Ford, who took my cat Bud for six months even though she had two of her own; Terrie McAlarney for caring for all 82 of my plants; Mike Ellis who lent me his personal computer when I was in the nursing home; my sister, Karen Perez, and my brother David Glines who were there every step of the way; Karen Mills-Bevers from Denver who visited me in the nursing home; Jack Wendt, a neighbor who scraped ice off my car, warmed up the car and walked me to it on snowy days; John Vernon who worked with me at the crack of dawn before I went to work so I could get my physical therapy done and improve my strength; Barbara Cash, a girlfriend since 9th grade, who came to visit me from Alaska when I was in the nursing home; Judi Maulsby, a fellow inpatient at Baylor, who has kept my spirits up through the years with her humor and has a way of making me laugh when I need to; Becky Taillon who helped me on weekends for three years with grocery shopping, errands, and anything I needed; Louise Hennig who took care of me in the nursing home and kept me company during the long days of confinement. Lori Fuller Payne who has been a true friend since we were kids; Mariel Fuller Rooney, a nurse and old neighbor from my younger days, who took such good care of me in the hospital in Flagstaff, Arizona; Sue Schnick, coworker at Littleton High School who checked in with me everyday at work to see how I was doing; Roy Payne who made justice prevail; Susan Davis, my boss at Littleton High School, who hired me in spite of my hobbling around on canes and never looked at me differently or treated me any differently due to my disability; Kaci Young who encourages and challenges me on a weekly basis to keep up my strength with exercises; Jane Hopkins, who keeps my neck massaged and comfortable; Roger Beach, who supported me through the years with my counseling career, keeping my spirits up and talking me through some dark days; Judy Hamrock who makes the best chicken soup. Thanks to Jon Chase for being such a supportive long-time friend who has kept John's musical creations and recordings alive.

And special thanks to my parents, Mary Ellen Glines and C.V. Glines who supported me in so many ways both financially, emotionally, unconditionally and to:

Mark Osmun, who extracted, organized, then gave a voice to my story—and along the way, chased off some lingering demons.

Most of all, I thank my husband, John Carpenter, who fills my life with joy, music and understanding and who makes our life together an adventure. Finding John again is the highlight of my life. I now know what it is to be truly loved for who you are and to be loved unconditionally. He helps me look for the rainbows after the storms. He is with me every step of the way, and sometimes those steps are slow ones.

About the Writer

Mark Osmun studied creative writing and English at George Mason University in Virginia, graduating *cum laude* in 1975. He attended two high schools: Punahou School in Honolulu and Langley High School in McLean, Virginia.

His writing career spans 40 years as a journalist, freelancer and author. He has worked as a foreign correspondent and travel writer for *The San Francisco Examiner*, west coast correspondent for *USA Today*, and is a past contributor to *Rolling Stone, Playboy, The Boston Globe, The San Francisco Chronicle, The Orange County Register, The Dallas Morning News, Sacramento Magazine, Honolulu Magazine, The Yacht Magazine, The Marin Independent Journal* and *The Runner Magazine.*

His two novels are the 2000 bestseller *Marley's Ghost* and *After the Bones.* Nonfiction works include *The Honolulu Marathon* and three biographies: *Dancer, V-Mail,* and *Bob Gong and the American Dream.* His 1985, six-part series for *The San Francisco Examiner* on South African apartheid became a finalist in the H.L. Mencken Awards of the Free Press Association. Writing has taken him to such places as Alaska, Scotland, Grenada, Costa Rica, Hawaii, South Africa, and throughout the United States.

For more on the author, please visit www.ravenideas.com . Older editions of *The Honolulu Marathon* and *Marley's Ghost* are available on amazon.com, but all his books are available at www.lulu.com.